TOP **10**
DUBAI
& ABU DHABI

LARA DUNSTON
&
SARAH MONAGHAN

EYEWITNESS TRAVEL

Left **An advertisement luring shoppers to buy Dubai's gold** Right **Windtowers along the Creek**

LONDON, NEW YORK,
MELBOURNE, MUNICH AND DELHI
www.dk.com

Design, Editorial and Picture Research
by Quadrum Solutions, Krishnamai, 33B,
Sir Pochkanwala Road, Worli, Mumbai, India

Printed and bound in China by Leo
Paper Products Ltd

14 15 16 17 10 9 8 7 6 5 4 3 2 1

First published in Great Britain in 2007
by Dorling Kindersley Limited
80 Strand, London WC2R 0RL
A Penguin Random House Company

Reprinted with revisions 2008, 2010,
2012, 2014

**Copyright 2007, 2014 © Dorling
Kindersley Limited, London**

A CIP catalogue record is available from
the British Library.

ISBN 978 1 4093 2681 6

Within each Top 10 list in this book, no
hierarchy of quality or popularity is
implied. All 10 are, in the editor's
opinion, of roughly equal merit.

MIX
Paper from
responsible sources
FSC™ C018179
www.fsc.org

Contents

Dubai & Abu Dhabi's Top 10

The information in this DK Eyewitness Top 10 Travel Guide is checked regularly.
Every effort has been made to ensure that this book is as up-to-date as possible at the time of
going to press. Some details, however, such as telephone numbers, opening hours, prices,
gallery hanging arrangements and travel information are liable to change. The publishers
cannot accept responsibility for any consequences arising from the use of this book, nor for
any material on third party websites, and cannot guarantee that any website address in this
book will be a suitable source of travel information. We value the views and suggestions
of our readers very highly. Please write to: Publisher, DK Eyewitness Travel Guides,
Dorling Kindersley, 80 Strand, London WC2R 0RL, or email: travelguides@dk.com.

Left **The impressive Jumeirah Beach Hotel** Right **A desert dune drive**

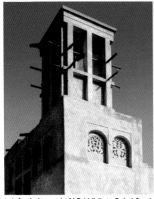

Left **A windtower in Al Fahidi** Right **Dubai Creek Golf & Yacht Club**

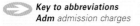
Key to abbreviations
Adm admission charges

3

DUBAI & ABU DHABI'S TOP 10

DUBAI & ABU DHABI'S TOP 10

🔟 Dubai & Abu Dhabi's Highlights

The Arabian emirates of Dubai and Abu Dhabi, the richest and most powerful of the seven city-states that make up the United Arab Emirates, offer the best of East and West – Arab culture, Bedouin heritage and Islamic architecture, alongside excellent shopping, sophisticated dining and luxurious hotels. Dubai is divided by its bustling Creek and skirted with white sand beaches, while Abu Dhabi is situated on a splendid Corniche.

1 Dubai Museum
Set in a well-preserved fort, the Dubai museum, with its whimsical dioramas *(below)* and fascinating displays, provides a comprehensive introduction to the city *(see pp8–9)*.

2 Dubai Creek
Criss-crossed by *abras* (water taxis) and *dhows* (old wooden boats) each day, this waterway *(below)* is Dubai's lifeblood *(see pp10–11)*.

3 Al Fahidi
The gypsum and coral courtyard houses *(left)* in this quarter were constructed by Persian merchants who settled here in the last century *(see pp12–13)*.

4 Jumeirah Mosque
Not only is this mosque *(right)* Dubai's most beautiful, it's the only mosque open to non-Muslims. A guided visit to learn about Islam and culture is a must *(see pp14–15)*.

5 Burj Al Arab
This iconic, attention-grabbing hotel *(above)* is certainly a sight you cannot miss. It's the world's tallest, all-suite hotel building *(see pp16–17)*.

Previous pages **The iconic Burj al Arab**

Abu Dhabi

EAST ROAD

AL ITTIHAD SQUARE

SHEIKH RASHID BIN SAEED AL MAKTOUM ST

AL NAHYAN
AL KARAMAH ST
SUDAN ST

Al
Manhal

Al
Tabbiyah

Al Lulu
Island

AL QURM CORNICHE ROAD
AL NAHR ROAD
AL NASR ST
ZAYED THE FIRST ST

KING KHALID BIN
ABDEL AZIZ ST

AL KHALEEJ
AL ARABI RD

Al
Khalidiyah

Al
Bateen

BAINUNAH STREET

Al
Khubeirah

Khor Al
Bateen

8

1 ⸺ miles ⸺ 0 ⸺ km ⸺ 1

Madinat Jumeirah (Dubai)

Shop for handicrafts, dine at a waterfront restaurant, see theatre or sip a cocktail as you enjoy the sunset at this Arabian-themed souq, entertainment and hotel complex *(see pp18–19)*.

Jumeirah
Mosque

4

Dubai
Museum **1** **3**

7 Dubai
Souqs

...eirah

ASL ROAD

Al Fahidi

Bur Dubai

Deira

Al Satwa

D73

D88

D90

D99

SHEIKH ZAYED ROAD

D78

2

Dubai
Creek

**Oud
Metha**

E66

E11

E13

Dubai Creek

Jaddaf

OUD METHA RD

Dubai Souqs

Bargain for gold, perfume, spices and textiles, or simply take in the heady atmosphere of Dubai's souqs *(see pp20–21)*.

Emirates
Palace

The jaw-dropping display of gold lining the walls *(right)* and Swarovski crystals dripping from the chandeliers at Abu Dhabi's Emirates Palace hotel make for an impressive sight *(see pp22–3)*.

The Islands

To the northeast of Abu Dhabi sit the three islands of Yas, Saadiyat and Al Maryah. With fantastic new attractions on Yas Island *(above)*, and many upcoming developments on the other two, these islands are much sought-after tourist destinations *(see pp24–5)*.

Desert Escapes

A visit to the UAE is incomplete without a desert experience. Stay at enchanting desert resorts Al Maha or Bab Al Shams or take a fun desert safari *(see pp26–7)*.

To enjoy the highlights at a more relaxed pace, spend a few days in Dubai, a day or two in Abu Dhabi and a day in the desert.

Dubai Museum

A visit to Dubai would be incomplete without a tour of this cleverly-planned museum. It offers a vivid picture of how Dubai has crammed into a third of a century what most cities achieve in several. Located near the creekside historic Al Fahidi district, the museum is housed within and beneath one of the city's oldest buildings, Al Fahidi Fort. It traces the city's meteoric development from small desert settlement to centre of the Arabian world for commerce, finance and tourism. Visit here to gain a sensory insight into traditions past and present.

Top 10 Features

1. Al Fahidi Fort
2. Barasti Windtower House
3. Bedouin Traditions Display
4. Multimedia Presentation
5. Old Dubai Souq Dioramas
6. Islamic School Dioramas
7. Desert at Night Exhibitions
8. Underwater Pearl Diving Exhibition
9. Archaeological Finds
10. Wooden Dhow

Bedouin wax figures

🗺 A souvenir area sells traditional Bedouin artefacts, but it's more fun, and cheaper, to bargain in the souqs.

☕ After your visit, retain the flavour of historic Dubai with lunch or coffee in the shady courtyard of nearby Basta Art Café *(see p71).*

- Map K2
- Al Fahidi Fort, Al Fahidi St
- 04 353 1862
- Open 8:30am–8:30pm Sat–Thu, 2:30–8:30pm Fri • Adm
- www.dubaitourism.ae

Al Fahidi Fort
Originally built in 1787, this fort, with its magnificent watch tower, was constructed to defend the Emiratis against invasion. Renovated in 1971, it now serves as a city museum.

Barasti Windtower House
The fort's courtyard houses a *barasti* (date palm frond) home *(below)* and windtower cooling system, common in the region up to the 1950s.

Bedouin Traditions Display
A gallery displays the costumes, jewellery, weapons and tools of the Bedouin people. A holographic video presentation of a tribe performing the ceremonial sword dance, the *Ardah*, is hypnotic.

Multimedia Presentation
A 10-minute film presentation, with archive footage, explains the development of modern Dubai from 1960 onward. The film takes you through a pictorial tour of Dubai's transformation over 40 years, decade-by-decade.

Old Dubai Souq Dioramas
Holographic technology combined with waxwork figures *(left)*, smells, sounds and archive footage transport you into the creekside souq of half a century ago.

Islamic School Dioramas
Young Emiratis recite the lines of the Koran *(right)* under the eye of their tutor in this reconstruction of a 1950s school.

Key to plans

  Ground floor
  Basement

Desert at Night Exhibitions
Learn how animals that live in the Arabian desert have adapted to cope with lack of water, extreme temperatures and shortage of food.

Underwater Pearl Diving Exhibition
This gallery explains the techniques used by pearl divers *(above)* who wore nose clips to descend to impossible depths.

Bedouin Culture
Bedu, the Arabic word from which the name Bedouin is derived, means "inhabitant of the desert". Bedouins would move from oasis to oasis by camel and would engage in small-scale agriculture. The hardships of the desert have imbued Bedouin culture with a strong honour code and a famous hospitality.

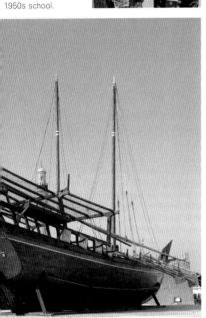

Wooden Dhow
A traditional Arab vessel, the *dhow (above)*, is on show at the museum's exit. For celestial navigation, sailors used the *kamal*, a device that determines latitude using the angle of the Pole Star above the horizon.

Archaeological Finds
Interesting artefacts from excavations of graves that

date back to 3,000 BC, such as fine copper and alabaster objects and pottery *(left)*, are on display.

Dubai and Abu Dhabi's Top 10

⒑⓪ Dubai Creek

Dubai Creek, fed by the waters of the Arabian Gulf, is the lifeblood of old and new Dubai – a vibrant mix of the past and the present. The contrast of traditional wooden dhows *being unloaded at the wharfage against stunning modern architecture, such as the glass dome-fronted Bank of Dubai (see p61) and the giant ball-topped Etisalat building, is fascinating. The two sides of the Creek are Deira (north) and Bur Dubai (south) and a walk along either is an enjoyable way to discover this multi-faceted city. Getting across the Creek is easy: the nearest bridge for cars is Maktoum Bridge but the cheapest and most authentic crossing has to be by* abra.

A creek cruise

🕐 By night illuminated *dhows* glide along the Creek.

🟠 Stop for a fresh juice at the stall by the entrance to the textile souq.

• Map K1–K6
• Abra Crossing: AED 1 each way • Creekside Park: 04 336 7633; Open 8am–11pm Sun–Wed, 2–11:30pm Thu–Sat; Adm; www.dm.gov.ae
• Sheikh Saeed Al Maktoum House: 04 393 7139; Open 8:30am–8:30pm Sat–Thu, 3–8:30pm Fri; Adm
• Heritage & Diving Village: Open 8:30am–10pm Sat–Thu, 3:30–10pm Fri • Bateaux Dubai: 04 399 4994; Open 7:45pm daily; www.bateauxdubai.com
• Al Mansour Dhow: Radisson Blu Hotel, Baniyas Road; 04 222 7171; departs 8:30pm
• Creek Cruises: 04 393 9860; www.creek cruises.com

Top 10 Features

1. Abra Trips
2. *Dhows*
3. Waterfront Heritage
4. Wharf Walk
5. Bur Dubai Waterfront
6. Bait Al Wakeel
7. The Diwan
8. Creekside Park
9. Creek Cruises
10. Bateaux Dubai

Abra Trips
Abras are flat-bottomed, open-sided water taxis *(right)* and are a breezy way to travel. Cram in with other passengers – the *abras* carry 40,000 people per day – and enjoy the great views.

Dhows
The *dhow* is the traditional sailing vessel of the Emirates. These beautiful wooden boats *(left)* are used for tourist rides as well as for trade.

Waterfront Heritage
In the Shindagha area near the Creek mouth you will find the restored house and museum of the late ruler Sheikh Saeed Al Maktoum and the Heritage and Diving Village *(below)*, which showcases Arabian culture.

Wharf Walk

It's worth taking an amble alongside the colourful painted *dhows* moored on the Creek on Baniyas Road. They arrive each day from India, Iran and Oman. You can wander by and watch their interesting wares being unloaded.

Bur Dubai Waterfront

The ruler's Diwan and historic architecture of "Old Dubai" can be enjoyed from the Deira side of the Creek *(above)*: windtowers, minarets and the domes of the Grand Mosque.

Bait Al Wakeel

Built in 1934, this was the Dubai office of the British East India Company *(below)*. It has been completely restored and now houses a restaurant.

The Diwan

With its modern white windtowers and imposing wrought-iron gates, the Diwan, or Ruler's Office, is impressive *(below)*.

Creek Cruises

Several tour operators offer creek cruises with buffet lunch or dinner and entertainment on traditional wooden sailing *dhows*. A sunset trip is a treat, especially if accompanied by live belly-dancing and Arabian music.

Bateaux Dubai

An evening on the Creek aboard the sleek, glass-encased Bateaux Dubai is a luxurious way to enjoy the views. Four-course dinners, white table linen and live piano music make this a romantic indulgence.

Creekside Park

A wonderful expanse of parkland, Creekside Park *(below)* stretches along the water's edge. Walk its length and enjoy the watery vistas or take a half-hour cable car ride along the length of the entire park.

History of Dubai Creek

Once a tiny fishing settlement sprawled around the palm-fringed mouth of the Creek, Dibei, as it was known in the 16th Century, owes its existence to the 14-km (9-mile) Dubai Creek which led into a natural harbour and established itself as a flourishing hub for entrepôt trade.

🔟 Al Fahidi

The old and atmospheric Al Fahidi quarter has benefited from extensive renovation work by Dubai Municipality. It gives a picturesque glimpse into the city's past in sharp contrast to the futuristic architecture and audacious construction projects elsewhere. Traditional sand, stone, coral and gypsum windtower houses, with elegant courtyards, can be explored as you wander the maze of shady narrow streets and alleys. The buildings have been restored to their original state, with Arabesque windows, decorative gypsum panels and screens. This area is now home to art galleries, museums and atmospheric cafés.

An Al Fahidi window

🕐 Set aside a couple of hours to fully see the Bastakiya quarter: late in the day, the golden light and long shadows add to the atmosphere.

🍴 For a light lunch, Basta Art Café offers healthy options such as fresh soups, salad and sandwiches.

• Map K2
• Sheikh Mohammed Centre for Cultural Understanding: 04 353 6666; www.cultures.ae
• Al Fahidi walking tours: 10am Sun & Thu; Adm
• Basta Art Café: 04 353 5071; Open 8am–10pm Sat–Thu
• Bastakiah Nights Restaurant: 04 353 7772; Open 12:30pm–11:30pm; DDD

Al Fahidi History

Bastak, in southern Iran, is the origin of the neighbourhood's previous name, Bastakiya. It was traders from Bastak who founded this area by the Creek in the early 1900s. Drawn by Dubai's liberal tax policies, they settled here permanently.

Traditional Architecture

The need to remain cool prompted the distinctive vernacular style of the windtower courtyard houses *(right)*. Thick walls and narrow windows with intricate Arabesque designs are characteristic.

Al Fahidi Fort

Now Dubai Museum *(see pp8–9)*, this Fort *(above)* dates back to 1787. A sighting recorded in 1822 calls this "a square castellated building, with a tower at one angle... with three or four guns mounted".

Old City Wall

Restoration work of the original 200-year-old city wall *(below)* has reinforced the importance of this section of the original city as a crucial defensive zone.

Sheikh Mohamed Centre for Cultural Understanding
Established in 1999 to promote understanding of traditional Emirati culture and Islam, this centre offers walking tours, Arabic courses and cultural awareness programmes. The building is a stunning architectural example of a courtyard house.

Stamp & Coin Museum
Philately House *(above)* hosts an exhibition of the history of post and currency in the UAE. It explores postal activities before the federation was born.

Majlis Gallery
Majlis means meeting place in Arabic and this bijou art gallery, with a central garden area, is constructed around a beautifully converted whitewashed Arabic house *(left)*. Local Emirati and expat artists feature alongside original pottery, ceramics, crafts and jewellery.

Basta Art Café
Set in a traditional courtyard of an Al Fahidi house, Basta Art Café *(below)* is a great spot to sit among flowering bougainvillea and enjoy lunch or a snack.

XVA Gallery, Café & Hotel
Enjoy contemporary art in galleries off the shady courtyard of this restored traditional house *(left)*. It also has a café and boutique hotel.

Bastakiah Nights Restaurant
This restaurant's *(right)* Arabian atmosphere is best experienced after dusk. The restored building has been traditionally furnished. Enjoy Arabic and Emirati food inside or on the rooftop.

Windtowers
Windtowers were the most distinctive architectural element of Arabic houses in the early 20th century. With four open sides, each of which was hollowed into a concave v-shape, wind-towers deflected the air down, cooling the rooms below. Water was thrown on the floor beneath the tower to cool the house further.

TOP 10 Jumeirah Mosque

Dubai's culture is rooted in Islam, a fact that touches all aspects of everyday life. Virtually every neighbourhood has its own mosque, but the jewel in the crown is undoubtedly Jumeirah Mosque. This fine example of modern Islamic architecture was built in 1998. It is a dramatic sight set against blue skies and is especially breathtaking at night, when it is lit up and its artistry is thrown into relief. Built of smooth white stone, the mosque, with its elaborately decorated twin minarets and majestic dome, is a city landmark and an important place of worship.

The mosque's interiors

🗨 Opposite the mosque is Japengo Café: it's a pleasant spot for a drink or light lunch on the terrace.

🏵 The mosque tours are intended to help visitors gain a real understanding of the Islamic faith, so make the most of the question time to find out what you would like to know. Photography is permitted.

• Map E4
• Jumeirah Road, Jumeirah
• 04 353 6666
• Mosque tours: Sat–Thu, 9:45am, AED 10, no booking required, meeting point outside mosque
• Sheikh Mohammed Centre for Cultural Understanding: www.cultures.ae
• Japengo Café: 04 345 4979, open 11am–1am, Sat–Fri

Top 10 Features

1. Mosque Architecture
2. Minarets
3. Mihrab
4. Minbar
5. "Open Doors, Open Minds" Tour
6. Five Pillars of Islam
7. Prayers
8. Ramadan
9. The Haj
10. Mosque Etiquette

Mosque Architecture

With its vast central dome (right), this mosque is inspired by the Anatolian style. The exterior is decorated in geometric relief over the stonework.

Mihrab

The attractive mihrab – the niche in the wall of this and every mosque that indicates the qibla, the direction one should face when praying – gives the impression of a door or a passage to Mecca (below).

Minarets

Two minarets (above) crown this mosque. The height of the tallest one – the highest point of the "House of Allah" – is determined by how far the call to prayer should be heard.

Minbar
The *minbar* (above) is the pulpit from which the *Imam* (leader of prayer) stands to deliver the *khutba* (Friday sermon).

"Open Doors, Open Minds" Tour
The "Open Doors, Open Minds" interactive guided mosque tour run by the Sheikh Mohammed Centre for Cultural Understanding, offers an opportunity to admire the subtle interior decoration and to gain insight into the Islamic religion *(right)*.

Five Pillars of Islam
The "Five Pillars of Islam" are: *Shahadah*, the belief in the oneness of God; *Salat*, the five daily prayers; *Zakat*, alms-giving; *Siyam*, self-purification and *Haj*, the pilgrimage to Mecca.

Prayers
The *adhan* (call to prayer) rings out five times a day – all able Muslims must supplicate themselves *(below)* to Allah by praying on a *musalla* (traditional mat).

The Haj
Every able-bodied Muslim is expected to make the annual pilgrimage to Mecca, in Saudi Arabia, once. Each year millions of Muslims from all over the globe do so to be forgiven of sins, to pray and to celebrate the glory of Allah.

Ramadan
During the holy month of Ramadan, Muslims abstain from food, drink and other physical needs. This is a time for purification and to focus on Allah.

Mosque Etiquette
Dubai may be cosmopolitan, but in keeping with mosque etiquette, you must dress conservatively to enter *(right)*. No shorts or sleeveless tops for either gender; women must wear a headscarf. Remove your shoes before entering.

Call to Prayer
Wherever you are in Dubai, you are likely to be within earshot of a mosque and to hear the daily calls to prayer *"Allahu akbar"* (God is great). Today, the modern-day call is transmitted through loudspeakers; in the past the muezzin made the call himself.

Non-Muslims are not allowed to enter mosques, but frequent cultural visitor tours permit you to enter this mosque's interior.

🔟 Burj Al Arab

So recognisable that it instantly became an international symbol for modern Dubai, the Burj Al Arab (meaning "Arabian tower"), completed in 1999, is an exclusive all-suite hotel. With its helipad on the 28th floor and a restaurant seemingly suspended in mid-air, at a soaring 321 m (1,053 ft), it takes the trophy for being the world's tallest all-suite hotel. Set on its own artificial island against the backdrop of the turquoise waters of the Gulf, it is dazzling white by day and rainbow-coloured by night when its façade is used as a canvas for spectacular light displays.

The Skyview bar

To visit the interiors, you must make a reservation for afternoon tea, cocktails or a meal. To do this, call 04 301 7600 or email BAArestaurants@ jumeirah.com

The dress code at the hotel means that you cannot wear jeans, t-shirts (collared shirts only), shorts, sandals (not in the case of women however), sports shoes or trainers.

- Map C1
- Jumeirah Rd, Dubai
- 04 301 7777
- Cheapest entry: high tea at Sahn Eddar (AED 285) or drinks package at Skyview Bar (AED 275 per person)
- Al Mahara: Open 12:30–3pm, 7pm–midnight; DDDDD
- Skyview Bar: Open noon–2am
- www.jumeirah.com

Top 10 Features

1. Architectural Inspiration
2. Exterior Architecture
3. Design Details
4. Interior Architecture
5. Fish Tanks
6. Lobby
7. Underwater Restaurant
8. Skyview Bar
9. Spa & Swimming Pool
10. Suites

1 Architectural Inspiration

The billowing sail of the traditional Arabian *dhow* was the inspiration for this contemporary architectural creation *(right)*. Access is via the causeway Rolls Royces for guests or by helicopter.

2 Exterior Architecture

The shore-facing façade of the Burj is covered by a stretched translucent fabric. This is Teflon-coated woven glass fibre. It is the first time such technology has been used in this way in any building worldwide.

3 Design Details

The interior oozes with exotic opulence, from the shell-shaped reception desk *(below)* to the gold-leafed surfaces. The upholstery is a riot of patterns and geometric designs.

Interior Architecture

The vast gold columns and many layers of floors rising up *(left)* from the lobby give a dizzying sensation.

Fish Tanks

The lobby boasts two-storey high tropical aquaria, carefully maintained by a dedicated in-house team.

Lobby

The upper lobby is an airy space of marbles, mosaics *(below)* and carpets in swirling patterns. There is an impressive multi-hued dancing fountain.

'Underwater' Restaurant

Eating at Al Mahara is like taking a submarine voyage. Dine on fresh seafood and watch exotic fish glide by in the aquarium *(below)*.

The Construction

The Burj Al Arab is said to be one of the most expensive buildings ever constructed and the cost has never been revealed. 250 foundation piles were driven 40 m (132 ft) deep into the seabed; 70,000 cubic m (2,472,026 cubic ft) of concrete and more than 9,000 tons of steel were needed to construct the tower structure; 43,446 sq m (467,648 sq ft) of glass cover the building; 30 different types of marble and 8,000 sq m (86,111 sq ft) of 22-carat gold leaf are incorporated in the decor.

Skyview Bar

This rooftop bar with its sky-high location offers spectacular vistas of the shimmering coastline. It is reached by an express panoramic lift. A must for cocktails at sunset.

Suites

The 202 duplex suites *(above)* are equipped with the latest remote technology, plus in-suite check-in and butlers. The two Royal Suites offer unsurpassed luxury, including a private cinema.

Spa & Swimming Pool

On the 18th floor is the Assawan Spa, a fitness facility with soothing ocean views. The decor is reminiscent of baths used by ancient Middle Eastern civilizations.

🔟 Madinat Jumeirah

The spirit of old Arabia is the inspiration for Madinat Jumeirah, an extravagant complex located on the beachfront comprising two luxury hotels, Al Qasr and Mina A'Salam, and the exclusive Dar Al Masyaf, 29 traditional courtyard summer houses. The charm of the place lies in its detailed Arabian architectural styling – sand-coloured windtowers, arches, stairways and terraces – as well as its ingenious construction around a series of man-made waterways. As a result, navigation around the resort is Venetian-style, in old-fashioned abras. There is an Arabian-style souq, restaurants and bars.

Souq Madinat Jumeirah

Top 10 Features

1. Souq Madinat Jumeirah
2. Madinat Amphitheatre
3. Madinat Theatre
4. Central Plaza: live music
5. Al Qasr Hotel
6. Mina A'Salam Hotel
7. Talise Spa
8. Arabian Waterways
9. Canal-side Eating
10. Koubba

If you get lost, ask for a resort map at any of the many information points. Guests can use a connecting board-walk to nearby Wild Wadi Water Park, Jumeirah Beach Hotel and Burj Al Arab.

For a real pick-me-up, try an espresso martini on the Koubba Bar terrace.

- Map C2
- Madinat Jumeirah, Al Sufouh Rd, Umm Suqeim, Dubai
- 04 366 8888
- Koubba Bar: Open 6pm–2am
- Zheng He's: Open noon–3pm & 7pm–11:30pm

Souq Madinat Jumeirah
This souq is a beautifully recreated Arabian market-place and as it is air-conditioned, is a delightful place to browse. On sale are Arabian handicrafts, carpets and curios, all, however, at tourist prices.

Madinat Amphitheatre
Built around a lagoon, this multi-purpose amphitheatre *(below)* seats over 1,000 people. It is designed in the style of an old fortress. The encircling citadel houses shops and restaurants.

Madinat Theatre
Host to the Dubai International Film Festival, the Madinat Theatre *(above)* – a 442-seat luxury venue – has provided this previously rather culture-starved city with a lively programme of opera, ballet, comedy and film.

Central Plaza
Follow the meandering paths through the souq past open-fronted shops and galleries to the central plaza, where you'll find A'Rukn – a street café with an Arabic twist – the perfect place to enjoy coffee and sample shisha.

Al Qasr Hotel
Al Qasr *(left)* is designed to reflect a Sheikh's summer residence. An opulent hotel, this quieter part of the whole complex is surrounded by water on a virtual island.

Mina A'Salam Hotel
Built in the style of a mythical Arabian city, this sea-facing hotel *(below)* is home to lively eating and drinking venues. All the rooms and suites have balconies.

Talise Spa
Relaxation is taken seriously in this tranquil oasis. The spa has 26 treatment rooms located on island clusters so you arrive by *abra*. Each treatment is described as "person-centric".

Canal-side Eating
Many of the res- taurants and bars have large terraces overlooking the tranquil waterways, making alfresco dining a delight thanks to Dubai's reliable sunshine. Zheng He's terrace is particularly charming.

Arabian Waterways
There's no doubt that the beautifully designed labyrinthine canals with *abras (above)* are magical and romantic. Only in the desert of Dubai could such a fantastic resort rise.

Dubai International Film Festival
Madinat Jumeirah is host to the Dubai International Film Festival (DIFF) which has seen celebrities such as Tom Cruise, George Clooney and Shahrukh Khan converge for a celebration of movie magic. Morgan Freeman expects that the festival will become "big enough to rival Cannes" in the years to come.

Koubba
Among Dubai's most romantic bars, Koubba *(left)* overlooks the stunning Al Qasr hotel and has views of the Arabian Gulf. Enjoy an evening on the balcony at this Arabian-themed nightspot *(see page 85)*.

TOP10 Dubai Souqs

Shopping in Dubai is a shopaholic's dream – there's almost nothing you can't buy here – but away from the air-conditioned marble-floored shopping malls is another experience: the souqs. Many of these, such as the gold, textile and spice souqs clustered beside the Creek, date back to Dubai's beginnings as a palm-fringed trading port. Exploring these through their warren-like alleyways is a delight and a visit to the UAE would be incomplete without spending time in at least some of these fascinating bazaars. Generally, each type of stall, be it spices, crafts, perfumes or clothing, are located close together, making it easy to spot a good deal. Bring cash and keep in mind that bargaining is expected.

Gold Souq's wares

⚙ Bargaining is expected in the souqs. Start at half of the initial price, more if you dare, and haggle with a smile until you reach a compromise.

Tax-free prices in Dubai tend to make luxury items such as CDs, perfume and electronic goods highly affordable.

🍽 There's a great choice of good-value Indian restaurants in the Bur Dubai souq area.

Most souqs tend to be open 10am–1pm & 4pm–10pm Sat–Thu, 2pm–10pm Fri
• www.dubaitourism.ae

Top 10 Features
1. Deira Gold Souq
2. Deira Spice Souq
3. Deira Perfume Souq
4. Deira Covered Souq
5. Naif Rd Souq, Deira
6. Bur Dubai Covered Souq
7. Bur Dubai Textile Souq
8. Karama "Souq"
9. Satwa "Souq"
10. Dubai Fish Souq

Deira Spice Souq
This tiny souq is a sensory delight. You can buy aromatic frankincense and myrrh (with charcoal burners for them), plus an array of spices *(below)* such as cloves, cardamom and cinnamon. Iranian saffron is good value, too.

Deira Gold Souq
This souq gleams with gold, silver and gems. Prices are competitive; dealers come in from around the globe and strict regulations are followed.

Deira Perfume Souq
Fascinating shops sell heavy exotic scents like jasmine, oudh, amber and rose and will also mix individual "signature scents". Traditional Arabian attars *(above)* are for sale alongside Western brands.

Deira Covered Souq
The Deira Covered Souq feels [mo]re Indian than Arabic, with a great [m]edley of merchandise on offer [in]cluding colourful and interesting [te]xtiles, spices, kitchenware, clothes [an]d henna being hawked.

Dubai and Abu Dhabi's Top 10

Naif Rd Souq, Deira
A kitsch faux desert fort houses this traditional-style souq *(below)*. You can find everything from cheap clothes and fake designerwear to children's toys and trinkets.

Bur Dubai Covered Souq
Beautifully restored, this creekside souq *(left)* is covered by an arched pergola. It makes for an atmospheric walkway lined with money lenders and little stalls.

Satwa "Souq"
This bustling street is a great place to rummage for cheaper products, such as fabrics, household items and electronics, as well as *majlis* cushion sets *(below)*.

Bur Dubai Textile Souq
Be warned, a visit here may prompt a visit to a tailor. Wonderful fabrics of every texture and colour imaginable from all over the world – silks, satins, brocades, linens and more *(above)*.

Karama "Souq"
This souq offers all kinds of "copy" items, especially watches and handbags. The quality of much of the merchandise, although fake, is astonishingly good.

Visit to a Tailor's
Dubai is a great place for tailoring, with textiles being so widely available. Various tailors' shops can be found around the Textile Souq, but also elsewhere in Satwa and Bur Dubai. Most will copy from an original item or photograph or you can select from an array of interesting pattern books.

Dubai Fish Souq
Hammour, a local [fis]h, is worth a buy. Here [yo]u can also barter for [fr]esh barracuda, giant [cr]ab *(above)*, lobster and [ot]her shellfish.

🔟 Emirates Palace

Abu Dhabi's stupendous Emirates Palace hotel dominates the horizon. While its staggering size is impressive, the lavish interior is breathtaking, with gold marble and crystal throughout. Owned by Abu Dhabi government and operated by Kempinski hotels, Emirates Palace was built over three years by the architects responsible for Claridge's in London. While the Burj Al Arab is touted as a "seven-star" hotel, a rating that doesn't exist, Emirates Palace classifies itself as just that, a "Palace", with the opulent furnishings of a royal palace, regal service and a palatial experience like no other.

The Triumphant Arch

🚗 If offered a buggy ride while wandering the grounds, it would be advisable to take it, as Emirates Palace is situated on a million sq m (over 10 million sq ft) of land.

☕ For a coffee or afternoon tea, call into Al Majlis coffee lounge or the Viennese style café. For a full meal, try Mezzaluna or Sayad *(see p93)*.

• Map N6
• The Corniche, Abu Dhabi
• 02 690 9000
• Taxi; if driving, there's valet parking
• Open 24 hours
• reservations.
emiratespalace@
kempinski.com
• www.emirates
palace.com

Top 10 Features

1. The Triumphant Arch
2. Palace Gardens & Fountains
3. Gold-plated Lobby
4. Domes
5. Palace Suites
6. Swarovski Crystal Chandeliers
7. Petrified Palm Trees
8. Algerian Sand Beach
9. Emirates Palace Theatre
10. *Majlis* with Arabian Horse Mural

1 The Triumphant Arch

Before entering Emirates Palace you'll be impressed by a majestic pink Triumphant Arch gate with a dome on top and a long and very grand driveway. The gate is usually closed. It is only opened for royalty and dignitaries on some special occasions.

2 Palace Gardens & Fountains

The exterior of the palace *(above)*, incorporating traditional Arabian elements, is painted to reflect the variations in colour of the Arabian sands. It is beautifully enhanced by its landscaped gardens and spectacular fountains.

3 Gold-plated Lobby

The opulence of the lobby's gold interior *(left)* is dazzling. Until Emirates Palace was built, Abu Dhabi was a modest city. This is the first time her wealth has been on display in such an ostentatious way.

Domes

There are 114 domes here. The most stunning is the Grand Atrium dome *(above)*, decorated with silver and gold glass mosaic tiles and a gold finial at its apex.

Palace Suites

Emirates Palace has 302 plush rooms and 92 sumptuously decorated Khaleej and Palace Suites. On the fifth floor is a reception for kings and heads of state and on the eighth are suites designed especially for the Gulf Rulers. The Saudi suite even has its own barbershop.

Swarovski Crystal Chandeliers

You'll notice the extravagant use of chandeliers *(above)* throughout the hotel – at Emirates Palace, they're used like light bulbs and appear to be sparkling everywhere.

Petrified Palm Trees

There are 8,000 trees within the hotel. The date palm *(below)*, a national icon, is everywhere. Some of the palm trees, petrified to preserve their natural beauty, look real and are very impressive.

Emirates Palace Theatre

Emirates Palace has given Abu Dhabi its first theatre, the largest in the UAE, with programs such as the Russian Ballet, Arabic orchestras and musical shows like "The Spirit of the Dance".

Algerian Sand Beach

The white sand of the 1.3 km- (1 mile-) long beach was imported from Algeria. A popular beach for swimming and cricket before Emirates Palace was built, it was felt the sand wasn't soft enough for royal feet!

Majlis with Arabian Horse Mural

The most impressive of the many plush public spaces here is the *majlis* (meeting area). It has a blue ceiling with frescoes and a magnificent mural of Arab stallions.

On a Scale Like No Other

The sheer scale of Emirates Palace impresses if nothing else. Ambassadors from 17 countries greet guests in the main lobby, and there are 170 chefs to keep you sated. There's no need to book or pay an entrance fee here. Simply show up and admire the structure.

Emirates Palace has a collection of some 1,002 chandeliers made with Swarovski's premier Strauss crystals.

TOP **The Islands**

The trio of islands to the northeast of the city centre – Yas, Saadiyat and Al Maryah – are the future of Abu Dhabi. The sparkling new developments on Yas Island, including the iconic Yas Marina Circuit and Ferrari World, are among the city's leading attractions. However, these are likely to be overshadowed by upcoming developments planned for Saadiyat Island, notably the Abu Dhabi Louvre and Guggenheim museums, designed by architects Jean Nouvel and Frank Gehry. Closer to Abu Dhabi is the new financial district on Al Maryah Island, ringed with gleaming skyscrapers and massive commercial complexes.

The stunning skyline of Al Maryah Island

🕐 There is plenty of accommodation on Yas Island. Rooms are especially sought-after during the F1 Grand Prix weekend in November, so book well ahead.

• Access Yas and Saadiyat Island from Abu Dhabi via Al Mina district or from the highway to Dubai.
• Road tours: Yas Leisure Drive offers an overview of the island's major sights.
• Taxi fares from Abu Dhabi: AED 40–50 to Yas Island, AED 25–30 to Saadiyat Island, AED 15–20 to Al Maryah Island
• www.yas.ae, www.saadiyat.ae, www.almaryahisland.ae

Top 10 Features

1. Yas Marina Circuit
2. Yas Viceroy Hotel
3. Yas Marina
4. Ferrari World
5. Yas Waterworld
6. Yas Beach
7. du Arena
8. Yas Links Golf Course
9. Manarat Al Saadiyat Gallery
10. Al Maryah Island

Yas Marina Circuit
The world's most spectacular Formula One venue, Yas Marina Circuit is set against a backdrop of massed yachts in the Yas Marina. The track runs directly beneath the stunning Yas Viceroy Hotel.

Yas Viceroy Hotel
This landmark five-star hotel *(below)* offers magnificent views of the racetrack and marina. The 217-m (712-ft) long glass-and-steel canopy with an integrated LED lighting system is distinctive, particularly after dark.

Yas Marina
A favoured playground of the rich in Abu Dhabi, Yas Marina *(above)* is lined with rows of swanky restaurants and bars. The water is dotted with innumerable million-dollar yachts, making for an impressive view.

Ferrari World

This massive indoor theme park, noted for being the largest in the world, has a range of Ferrari-themed attractions *(above)*, including the world's fastest rollercoaster and a fantastic F1 simulator. The park offers a host of rides for families and children.

Yas Waterworld

With plenty of thrills and spills like the stomach-churning Jebel Drop, Yas Waterworld is a great place for adrenaline junkies. There are more moderate rides, and the pools and slides are for all ages and inclinations.

Yas Beach

Lounge on a deck chair with *sheesha* by your side at this gorgeous white-sand beach *(above)*. The attractive beach-café and bar also serves food and drinks.

du Arena

This state-of-the-art outdoor arena *(below)*, complete with a cooling system for the hot summer months, is Abu Dhabi's principal concert venue. Well known international celebrities perform here regularly.

Yas Links Golf Course

The Gulf's first Links course *(below)*, conceived by the celebrated designer Kyle Phillips, offers an excellent 18-hole champion-ship course that runs along the beautiful Yas Island shoreline.

Manarat Al Saadiyat Gallery

A modest but interesting gallery, with exhibitions that showcase the grandiose plans for Saadiyat Island. However, most of these developments, such as the Abu Dhabi Louvre Museum, are yet to leave the drawing board.

Al Maryah Island

This is Abu Dhabi's glitzy new financial district. Its incredible skyscrapers and office blocks can be seen from downtown, rising above the water.

🔟 Desert Escapes

The Emirates' desert is sublime in parts and a trip here is incomplete without experiencing its myriad textures and colours. Not far out of the cities, camels graze on desert grass. If you don't have a 4WD and off-road driving skills, the best way to experience the desert is at the magical desert resorts Al Maha or Bab Al Shams, or on a popular desert safari. While desert safaris are touristy, they're lots of fun and allow you to tick off a range of experiences you otherwise wouldn't get a chance to do. If you have time, stay overnight, sleep under the stars and enjoy the silence.

An Arabian camel

A magical desert sunset

⏱ Unless you want to experience the scorching heat for which the UAE is infamous, visits to the desert are best done in spring, autumn or winter – never summer!

• *Al Maha Resort: Dubai – 04 832 9900; www.al-maha.com*
• *Arabian Adventures: Dubai – 04 303 4888/343 9966, Abu Dhabi – 02 691 1711; Open 9am–6:30pm; Prices start at AED 335 per person; www.arabian-adventures.com*
• *Dream Days: 04 800 2080*
• *Bab Al Shams Desert Resort & Spa: 04 809 6100; www.meydanhotels.com/babalshams*

Top 10 Features

1. The Desert
2. Desert Safaris
3. Bedouin Tents
4. Dune Bashing
5. Quad Biking
6. Camel Riding
7. Belly Dancing
8. Bedouin Feast
9. Bab Al Shams Desert Resort & Spa
10. Al Maha Resort & Spa

1 The Desert

The UAE is all desert, apart from Al Ain's lush date palm oases, the Hajar mountains and rocky east coast. There are stunning dunes *(below)* dotted with camels on the roads to Hatta and Al Ain, but the most spectacular dunes are in the Liwa Oasis.

2 Desert Safaris

Tour agencies like Arabian Adventures organize exciting desert safaris. These may include an exhilarating desert drive in a 4WD *(above)*, falconry displays, sandboarding, a sunset camel ride, Arabic buffet and belly dancing.

3 Bedouin Tents

Traditional chocolate-coloured goat- and camel-hair tents dot the desert dunes in winter. Emiratis love to get away from the cities and take their children camping so they don't forget their heritage.

 To avoid dehydration in the desert, drink plenty of water. Protect yourself from the sun by slathering on sunscreen.

Dune Bashing
Experience an exhilarating "dune bashing" session – a white-knuckle 4WD desert drive across the monstrous sand dunes.

Quad Biking
Quad biking over the dunes is a popular and thrilling way of seeing the desert. This activity, however, is not for the faint-hearted and safety equipment must be worn.

Camel Riding
Get up-close-and-personal with this local beast of burden. Nothing is quite like a camel ride *(above)* along spectacular dunes at sunset on a desert safari.

Belly Dancing
Belly dancing is known as Oriental dancing in the Middle East. Try to pick up some moves from the dancer at the desert safari *(below)* – she may even pull you up for a shimmy.

Bedouin Feast
Try a delicious Arabic buffet *(below)*, such as the Bedouin feast at Bab Al Shams' Al Hadheerah Desert Restaurant. Try local specialities including roasted baby camel.

Al Maha Resort & Spa
Book a private and romantic tent-like luxury suite, and get your own plunge pool with the golden desert as your "backyard".

Bab Al Shams Desert Resort & Spa
The palm-shaded gardens and trickling ponds make this desert resort *(below)* enchanting. A wonderful infinity pool overlooks the desert. Enjoy falconry here.

Liwa Oasis
The most spectacular desert scenery can be enjoyed at Liwa Oasis, just a few hours drive from Abu Dhabi. The sand dunes of the Liwa are the prettiest-coloured, in shades of peach and apricot. They are also the largest in the UAE – best appreciated shortly after sunrise or sunset.

Following pages: **Camels being led across the desert sands**

Left **Camels grazing in the desert** Right **Henna application**

🔟 Culture & Tradition

1 Bedouin Society
The semi-nomadic lifestyle of the Bedu tribes – most of whom spent the harsh summers inland at the cool date-palm oases and their winters fishing by the sea – is a source of pride for Emiratis. ⊗ *Visit the Heritage Villages in Dubai (see p67) and Abu Dhabi (see p89) for a glimpse into the Bedouin culture.*

2 The Camel
Mainstay of the Bedouin's nomadic life, the camel enabled tribes to move their possessions from coastal villages to inland oases. Camel's milk quenched their herders' thirst when water wasn't found, while the fur was used to make tents, textiles, rugs, bags and cloaks. ⊗ *Ride a camel at the Heritage and Diving Village in Dubai (see p67).*

3 The Arabian Horse
Beloved by the Bedouin for their elegance and valued for their strength and sturdiness, the Arabian horse is one of the world's oldest and purest of breeds due to the Bedouin's careful inbreeding, practiced for centuries. ⊗ *Appreciate the beauty of the Arabian horse on display at the Heritage and Diving Village (see p67) during Eid and Shopping Festivals.*

4 Falconry
In the past, falcons were used by Bedu to capture small birds and hares. Today, Emirati men still train their falcon daily. Some desert resorts and safaris display falconry. ⊗ *Abu Dhabi Falcon Hospital: Swehan Rd; tours 10am & 2pm Sun–Thu, book in advance; www.falcon hospital.com*

5 The Date Palm
Dates were essential for desert survival. They were used to create *tamr,* a preserve, which helped sustain the Bedu over long journeys. There are over 50 date varieties in the UAE. ⊗ *Bateel (see p37) sells good dates.*

6 Fishing and the *Dhow*
Historically, fishing, *dhow* building and pearl diving were the main occupations along the coastal settlements. Today, Emiratis still use the old wooden *dhow* boats for fishing, trading and tours. ⊗ *Visit dhow-building wharves in Abu Dhabi (see p90).*

7 Poetry, Dance & Song
Emirati poetry takes many forms, from the romantic *baiti* style to the vernacular *nabati*

An Emirati wedding procession

Camel's milk is more nutritious than cow's milk. You can buy it at the local supermarkets in Dubai and Abu Dhabi.

An Emirati with his falcon

poetry. Wedding processions are an occasion for song and dance. Songs and group dances such as the *ayyalah* and *liwa* celebrate bravery in war and at sea. ◎ *Enjoy traditional performances at the Heritage and Diving Village (see p67) during Eid and the Dubai Shopping Festival.*

Rifle-throwing
Prior to Federation there was periodic warring between tribes, and Bedu were respected for how they handled weapons. These days, young Emirati men practice throwing their rifles high in the air while dancing and clapping. ◎ *Watch gun-throwing competitions at the Heritage and Diving Village (see p67) during Eid and the Dubai Shopping Festival.*

Traditional Dress
Women wear a black cloak-like *abaya* and black *shayla* to cover their hair. Men wear a white *dishdasha* and a white or checked *gutra* (head scarf) with a black *agal* to hold it in place.

Henna
Intricate henna patterns were painted on pottery across the Middle East in Neolithic times, around 9000 BC. Today, Emirati women have henna designs painted on their hands and feet for weddings and other celebrations. ◎ *Get henna designs at "henna tents" in shopping malls.*

Moments in History

1 5000 BC: Abu Dhabi settlement
Date stones on Dalma Island and flint tools on Merawah Island attest to human life in Abu Dhabi in 5110 BC.

2 AD 700: Islam arrives
The Umayyads bring Islam and Arabic to Arabia.

3 1507: European traders reach the Gulf
Portuguese invasion of Gulf islands and the east coast paves way for British, French and Dutch trading ships.

4 1793: Al Bu Falah tribe settles in Abu Dhabi
Al Bu Falah and Al Nahayan tribes settle in Abu Dhabi.

5 1833: Al Maktoum tribe arrives in Dubai
Under leadership of Maktoum bin Buti Al Maktoum, Al Maktoum tribe settles at the mouth of Dubai Creek.

6 1894: Tax-free trading
Dubai first introduces tax exemptions for foreigners. The Persians are the first expats.

7 1930s: Pearling trade collapses
The Gulf pearling trade collapses when the Japanese develop cultured pearling.

8 1950s: Discovery of oil
Oil is discovered in Abu Dhabi in 1958 and Dubai in 1966, changing fortunes.

9 1971: UAE established
UAE Federation forms from the seven emirates, with Sheikh Zayed bin Sultan Al Nahayan, ruler of Abu Dhabi, as President.

10 2004: Death of Sheikh Zayed
UAE goes into mourning with the death of visionary leader Sheikh Zayed, and in 2006, the death of Sheikh Maktoum.

➔ *When Marco Polo visited Dubai in 1580, he described it as a bustling seaport that was rich from its trade in pearls.*

Left **Dolphins near Saadiyat Island** Centre **Sir Bani Yas Island** Right **Ferrari World, Yas Island**

🔟 Audacious Projects

1 Sir Bani Yas Island
This cone-shaped island in the Arabian Gulf has been transformed into an extraordinary conservation project open to tourists. If you are lucky you may spot African giraffes and ostriches, llamas from Peru and even the more local Arabian oryx. ◈ *Off the Abu Dhabi coast • 02 801 5400 • www.desertislands.com*

2 The Palm Jumeirah
This palm-shaped island may qualify for the "Eighth Wonder of the World" tag. It is one of the largest man-made developments on earth and is visible from space. Housing premium location property, the Palm is also home to the enormous Atlantis, The Palm hotel *(see p44)*. Two even bigger palm island projects, Palm Jebel Ali and Palm Deira, are under construction. ◈ *Map B1 • Dubai • www.thepalm.ae*

3 Meydan City
This giant development is themed around the national love of equestrian pursuits. Its centrepiece is the state-of-the-art Meydan Racecourse, which has the world's largest grandstand, a turf track, an all-weather track and a five-star hotel. The venue hosts the Dubai World Cup, the famous racing challenge *(see p35)*. Training facilities, malls, offices and a marina are planned. ◈ *Map D2 • Dubai • www.meydan.ae*

4 Ski Dubai
The largest indoor snow park in the world, this cavernous space contains 6,000 tonnes of manufactured snow, and houses a penguin enclosure. Five runs vary in difficulty, the longest being almost a quarter of a mile (400 m), making it the world's first indoor black run. ◈ *Map C2 • 04 409 4000 • Mall of the Emirates, Al Barsha, Dubai • www.skidxb.com*

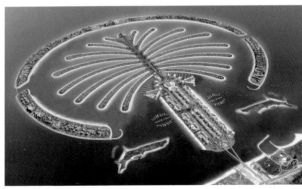

The amazing Palm Jumeirah project

Yas Island

This desert island is being transformed into Abu Dhabi's top leisure destination. Home to the Yas Marina Circuit – where the Formula 1 Grand Prix takes place – as well as a marina, hotels and golf courses. The main attraction is Ferrari World, the world's biggest indoor theme park, where Formula Rossa, the fastest roller coaster, is located. ◈ *Dubai • www.yasisland.ae*

Masdar City

Abu Dhabi's "green city", when completed, will rely entirely on solar energy and other renewable energy sources, with a zero-carbon, zero-waste policy. The city is being constructed at a cost of some $22 billion at a site beside Abu Dhabi International Airport. Once finished, it will host the headquarters of the International Renewable Energy Agency. ◈ *Abu Dhabi • www.masdar.ae*

Dubai Festival City

A "city within a city", this huge waterfront lifestyle resort extends 2 miles (4 km) along the Creek. It comprises a mind-boggling 20,000 homes, with schools, malls, hotels, a marina, waterside restaurants, and event and leisure facilities, including a golf course. ◈ *Map E3 • Dubai • www.dubaifestivalcity.com*

Burj Khalifa

At over 800 m (2,600 ft), the Burj Khalifa (formerly known as the Burj Dubai) is the world's tallest tower. It took over five years of construction by more than 7,500 workers to reach completion in 2009. The tower houses the Armani Hotel, an observation deck and some of the world's fastest elevators. In front of it, the Dubai Fountain *(see p73)* is the setting for a sound and light show.

Burj Khalifa, the world's tallest tower

Dubai Infrastructure

With so much development planned for the near future, the city's transport infrastructure is crucial. Two of the three major projects have been completed. The first saw the expansion of Dubai International Airport, creating an exclusive terminal for Emirates (Dubai's airline). The second was the development of the Dubai Metro, the world's longest automated unmanned metro, linking various parts of the city with an under- and overground railway. The third project will be a freight-focused airport on the city outskirts at Jebel Ali.

Saadiyat Island

Set to become a major tourist destination for Abu Dhabi, this island is scheduled to be constructed over the next few years. It will be home to some 150,000 people and several world-class museums, including the Guggenheim Abu Dhabi, to be designed by Frank Gehry, a branch of the Louvre *(see p91)*, and a Biennale Park with 19 pavilions.

Left **Exhibition at Gallery Isabelle van den Eynde** Centre **Pop art at Art Space** Right **The Third Line**

TOP 10 Art Galleries

The Third Line
This sleek gallery shows provocative and playful work by artists from around the Gulf. Exhibitions change every few weeks, launched by champagne openings. ◈ *Map C2 • Al Quoz industrial area, off Interchange 3, Dubai • 04 341 1367 • Open 10am–7pm Sat–Thu; Call ahead • www.thethirdline.com*

XVA
This superb art gallery is set in a stylish boutique hotel in a restored traditional house. Its courtyard café is also used as an exhibition space *(see p13)*.

Majlis Gallery
Dubai's oldest commercial art gallery focuses on Arabian and Middle Eastern themed work. Browse for good prints, ceramics and sculpture here *(see p13)*.

Art Space
With a mission to nurture local talent, this gallery has hosted great exhibitions by Middle Eastern and Emirati artists, like Mohammed Kanoo's playful pop art. ◈ *Map D2 • Gate Village, DIFC • 04 323 0820 • Open 10am–8pm Sun–Thu*

Gallery Isabelle van den Eynde
Check out the provocative paintings, photography and mixed media predominantly by Middle Eastern artists. Standout shows include Iranian artist Ramin Haerizadeh's photo-manipulation using his own face to recreate themes from Persian theatre. ◈ *Map C2 • Al Quoz industrial area, off Interchange 3, Dubai • 04 340 3965 • Open 10am–7pm Sat–Thu • www.ivde.net*

The Courtyard: Total Arts and The Courtyard Gallery
The highlights at this rather whimsical-looking Mediterranean-style complex are two wonderful galleries – Dariush Zandi's Total Arts at the Courtyard and Samia Saleh and Louis Rady's lovely Courtyard Gallery and Café. ◈ *Map C2 • Al Quoz industrial area, off Interchange 3, Dubai • Total Arts 04 347 0909; The Courtyard Gallery 04 347 5050 • www.courtyard-uae.com*

Green Art Gallery
This established commercial gallery in Al Quoz showcases the work of Emirates-based as well as international artists who are inspired by the heritage,

An exhibit at XVA

Artwork at Hemisphere Gallery

cultures and environment of the Middle East. There is a season of changing exhibitions from October to May. 🅢 *Map C2 • Al Quoz industrial area, off Interchange 3, Dubai • 04 346 9305 • Open 10am–7pm Sat–Thu • www.gagallery.com*

Ghaf Art Gallery

This gallery features regular monthly exhibitions of work from local as well as well-known international artists. 🅢 *Map Q4 • Khaleej Al Arabi St • 02 665 5332 • Open 10am–8pm Sat–Thu*

Folklore Gallery

One of the best places to find works of art and craft from across the region, as well as handmade greeting cards, Turkish bookmarks, prints and handblown glass. Gift items are also available. 🅢 *Map P4 • Zayed 1st Street, Al Khalidiya • 02 666 0361 • Open 9am–9pm Sat–Thu*

Hemisphere Gallery

Abu Dhabi's foremost art gallery is set in the most unlikely location, among the shops and laundries around the Russian embassy. The gallery exhibits a variety of styles and works by expat artists as well as running painting courses and workshops. 🅢 *Map P2 • Off Khalifa St, near the Russian Embassy, Abu Dhabi • 02 676 8641 • Open 9:30am–1:30pm & 3–9pm Sat–Thu*

Top 10 Festivals & Events

1 Dubai Shopping Festival
Sales and shows. 🅢 *Citywide • Dec–Feb • www.mydsf.ae*

2 Global Village
Multicultural bazaar and fun fair. 🅢 *Map C3 • Dubailand, Emirates Road • Dec–Feb 4pm–midnight • www.globalvillage.ae*

3 Dubai International Film Festival
Glam galas and film screenings. 🅢 *Map C2 • Madinat Jumeirah, Um Suqueim, Dubai • Dec • www.dubaifilmfest.com*

4 Dubai International Jazz Festival
Global jazz gigs on the grass. 🅢 *Map B2 • Dubai Media City, Um Suqueim, Dubai • Mar • www.dubaijazzfest.com*

5 Dubai Marathon
Compete or simply run for fun! 🅢 *From Sheikh Zayed Rd to Jumeirah Beach Rd • Jan • www.dubaimarathon.org*

6 Dubai World Cup
World's richest horse-racing cup. 🅢 *Map D3 • Meydan racetrack, Dubai • Feb–Mar • www.dubaiworldcup.com*

7 Dubai Desert Classic
Renowned golf players participate. 🅢 *Map B2 • Mar • www.dubaidesertclassic.com*

8 Dubai Tennis Championships
Catch top tennis seeds in action. 🅢 *Feb–Mar • www. dubaiduty freetennischampion ships.com*

9 Art Dubai
An annual contemporary art fair. 🅢 *Madinat Arena • Mar • www.artdubai.ae*

10 UAE Desert Challenge
A 4-day motor rally through the desert. *• www. abudhabidesertchallenge.com*

The winter months of December to March are crammed with festivals and events.

Dubai and Abu Dhabi's Top 10

Left **The amazing Ibn Battuta Mall** Right **Abu Dhabi's Marina Mall**

Shopping Malls & Souqs

The Dubai Mall
Next to the world's biggest tower sits the world's largest shopping mall. This monument to consumerism houses over 1,000 stores, not to mention an ice rink, an aquarium and a vast cinema and entertainment complex. The mall also boasts over 150 food outlets offering everything from fine dining to casual eateries *(see p75)*.

Mall of the Emirates
Over 520 stores, including a swish Harvey Nichols, make this the city's most sumptuous mall. If you're in a rush, use the mall's website to create an itinerary identifying the most direct route to the shops you wish to visit *(see pp78–81)*.

Burjuman Mall
This glamorous mall houses exclusive designer stores such as Chanel, Dior and Kenzo, and jewellers like Cartier and Tiffany. There's a Saks Fifth Avenue, the second largest outside the USA, and shops selling books, music, perfumes and cosmetics *(see p70)*.

Deira City Centre
This mall may not be as spectacular as the newer shopping centres, but it's a local favourite. While you'll find all the usual Dubai stores here, most visitors come mainly for the excellent people watching *(see p62)*.

Dubai Festival Centre
This waterfront development offers a French Riviera-style marina, excellent shopping and al fresco dining. It has more than 400 shops, including a huge Marks & Spencer, Paris Gallery, IKEA and Toys"R"Us *(see p62)*.

Ibn Battuta Mall
One look at the five themed malls within this mall and you won't regret your long drive! The decor for each is inspired by the countries that Arabia's own Marco Polo, Ibn Battuta, travelled to: Tunisia, Egypt, Persia, India and China *(see p82)*.

Dalma Mall
Once Abu Dhabi's biggest mall, Dalma Mall has something for everyone. Anchor stores include Carrefour, Home Center, Centrepoint and Matalan. There's also a 14-screen cinema and a

The posh interiors of Burjuman

36

For Emiratis, shopping malls are about socializing as much as they are about shopping.

Dalma Mall

Fun City. It is close to Mohammed Bin Zayed City.
🕭 Abu Dhabi-Tarif Hwy • 02 550 6111
• Open 10am–10pm Sun–Wed, 10am–midnight Thu–Sat • www.dalmamall.ae

Marina Mall
This glamorous mall has over 300 shops. Expect big name brands, exclusive stores such as Rolex and Tiffany & Co, and traditional Arabian perfume, sweets and clothes shops. The excellent cafés include Hediard from Paris (see p92).

Galleria
One of the city's newest consumer additions, Galleria houses boutique stores owned by world-class luxury brands. It is set across three floors (see p92).

Souk Al Bahar
Just over the waterway from The Dubai Mall sits a more Arabic-themed affair with various boutique and antique shops. There is also an excellent selection of eateries and bars (see p74).

Top 10 Shops

1 Damas
Visit the Gulf's largest jeweller for a huge selection of dazzlers (see p62).

2 Paris Gallery
This store has an enticing array of make-up and perfume at bargain prices (see p62).

3 Sharaf DG
A digital and electronics retailer – the first stop for gadget lovers (see p62).

4 Bateel
Buy date goodies such as chocolate-coated dates or date jam as gifts. 🕭 Map J3
• Burjuman Mall, Sheikh Khalifa Bin Zayed Rd, Dubai
• 04 355 2853

5 Villa Moda
An elegant place for exclusive designerwear, from Alexander McQueen to Stella McCartney (see p36).

6 Mumbai Se
A must-visit for glam Bollywood-style clothing and high-end Indian fusion fashion. 🕭 Map C6 • The Dubai Mall, Dubai • 04 434 0626

7 Azza Fahmy Jewellery
Inimitable jewellery combining Arabic calligraphy and Islamic motifs. 🕭 Map D6
• Jumeirah Emirates Towers Boulevard, Sheikh Zayed Rd, Dubai • 04 330 0346

8 Amzaan
Creative Dubai designers share space with hip foreign labels (see p70).

9 Sauce
You'll love the chic accessories and fashion. 🕭 Map D4 • Village Mall, Jumeirah Rd, Dubai • 04 344 7270

10 Candylicious
The world's biggest sweet shop. 🕭 Map C6 • The Dubai Mall, Dubai

Dubai and Abu Dhabi's Top 10

 Get a copy of Emirates Woman magazine, the leading fashion title, when you arrive in town for more on local style.

37

Left **Dazzling gold bangles** Centre **Arabian antique lamp** Right **Beautiful designer textiles**

ᴱ10 Things to Buy

Gold
Dubai is "the City of Gold". The Gold and Diamond Park glitters with ornate jewellery. Gold is sold by weight; intricate designs are more expensive.
Ⓢ *Map C2 • Sheikh Zayed Rd, Interchange 4, Dubai • 04 347 7788 • Open 10am–10pm Sun–Thu, 10am–midnight Sat–Fri • www.goldanddiamondpark.com*

Carpets
The UAE is the best place to buy Persian carpets outside of Iran. A discerning market ensures the best quality rugs come here while no tax keeps prices low. Shop around and bargain hard but most of all, enjoy the tea – the ritual is half the fun of it.

Arabian "Antiques" & Handicrafts
Arabian "antiques" include brass coffee pots, engraved trays and framed *khanjars* (daggers). You'll also find traditional Emirati handicrafts such as woven baskets, embroidery and red striped textiles made into camel bags and rugs. Moroccan lanterns, Turkish and Persian miniature paintings and Indian cushion covers are also popular.

Arabian Attars & Perfumes
The heady aromas of exotic Arabian *attars* (perfume oils) are an acquired smell. Many women buy them for the beautiful jewel-encrusted bottles. If offered *oud* (fragrant wood) in an incense

Traditional Bedouin jewellery

burner, don't forget to waft the smoke under your arms – it is used traditionally as a deodorant.

Bedouin Jewellery
Much of the old silver Bedouin jewellery comes from Oman, Yemen, Afghanistan and India, but only experts can tell. Expect to find chunky bangles, necklaces, earrings and rings, engraved and intricately set with gemstones, cowrie shells and dangling little bells.

Pink Sushi Designs
This local label features cute handbags and quirky skirts made using the *gutra*, the red and white checked Emirati head-dress. They are available from various stores, including Amzaan *(see p70)* and Sauce *(see p37)*.

Electronics/Digital Products

The range of electronic products is enormous – if there's a gadget on the market, you'll get it here. The tax-free environment means prices are low, but competition (don't be surprised to see a dozen electronics stores all in a row) means amazing prices and bargains if you shop around.

Global Designer Brands

Being tax-free, the world's best designers and exclusive labels here go for a fraction of the price they do elsewhere. ◈ *Map P2 • Madinat Zayed neighbourhood, Abu Dhabi • Open 10am–1pm & 4–10pm Sat–Thu, 4–10pm Fri*

Arabic & Middle Eastern Music

You'll hear music everywhere in the Emirates, whether it's traditional songs performed at a heritage village, Egyptian pop on the radio, a Moroccan band in a restaurant or contemporary Arabic lounge at a hip bar. Buy Middle Eastern music at Virgin Megastore at the malls or at a music shop in the souqs.

Fun Souvenirs

Pick up some kitsch key rings and ashtrays, mosque-shaped alarm clocks, cuddly camels that play Arabic music when you squeeze them, or even Burj Al Arab paperweights.

Humorous souvenirs

Top 10 Places to Buy Arabian Handicrafts & Souvenirs

1 Al Jaber Gallery
An Aladdin's cave selling exotic Arabian handicrafts and souvenirs (see p62).

2 Al Orooba Oriental
The finest carpets and kilims, along with antique prayer beads, silver jewellery and ceramics.

3 Showcase Antiques Art and Frames
A collection of old Bedouin jewellery, khanjars and coffee pots. ◈ *Map C2 • Jumeirah Rd, Umm Suqeim, Dubai • 04 348 8797 • Open 10am–1pm & 4–10pm Sat–Thu, 4–8pm Fri*

4 Pride of Kashmir
Renowned for soft pashmina shawls, carpets, cushions and throws (see p62).

5 Gallery One Fine Art Photographs
Black and white photographs of Dubai's iconic symbols. ◈ *Map C2 • Madinat Jumeirah, Dubai • 04 368 6055*

6 Khalifa Centre
Bargain for carpets and handicrafts here (see p92).

7 Allah-din Shoes
Beautiful sequinned slippers. ◈ *Map J1 • Bur Dubai Souq, Dubai, by the abra dock • 050 515 4351*

8 Camel Company
Shop for cute camel gifts. ◈ *Map C2 • Madinat Jumeirah, Dubai • 04 368 6048*

9 Ajmal
Arabian attars and oils in ornate bottles (see p62).

10 Bateel
Buy dates in a variety of beautifully-packaged gift boxes (see p37).

Dubai Duty Free at Dubai Airport has a wonderful range of well-priced souvenirs if you forget something.

Left **A lit-up Almaz by Momo** Centre **Live music at Tagine** Right **A taste of Persia at Shabestan**

Top 10 Middle Eastern Restaurants

Tagine
A vast wooden door leads you to a sumptuous cultural dining experience at Tagine (a Moroccan clay cooking pot) with live music, candlelight and an exotic decor. Mezze or harira soup for starters can be followed by kebabs, aromatic tagines and couscous dishes *(see p83).*

Marrakech
The mosaic-tiled walls, soft lighting and graceful arches create a strong North African atmosphere, completed by live oud and Moroccan classics like couscous royale and tagine kofta. Ask to sit in one of the half-moon booths. *Map C5 • Shangri-La Hotel, Sheikh Zayed Road • 04 405 2703 • Open 7pm–midnight • DDDDD*

Zahr el Laymoun
Featuring a lovely terrace overlooking the Dubai Fountain, this restaurant offers healthy Lebanese cooking, with superb fruit juices; tasty kebabs and great desserts. *Map C6 • Souk Al Bahar, Downtown Burj Khalifa • 04 448 6060 • Open 10am–midnight daily • DDD*

Shabestan
Award-winning, classic Persian cuisine is combined with spectacular creek views and superlative service at Shabestan. Try one of the traditional kebabs served with saffron rice. *Map K2 • Radisson Blu Hotel • 04 222 7171 • Open 12:30–3:15pm & 7:30–11pm • DDD*

Awtar
A late dinner here is a spectacle with a nightly performance by an exuberant bellydancer. Friendly Lebanese waiters add to the vibrant atmosphere. The mezze is excellent. *Map J6 • Grand Hyatt Dubai • 04 317 2222 • Open 12:30–3pm & 7pm–3am Sun–Fri • DDD*

Al Nafoorah
Don't judge Al Nafoorah by its staid atmosphere – the Lebanese food is fresh, delicious and generous. You'll find an extensive menu, with great desserts. *Map D6 • Emirates Towers, Sheikh Zayed Road • 04 319 8088 • Open 12:30–4pm & 7pm–midnight • DD*

Mezlai
Apart from being UAE's only restaurant that serves Emirati food, this is also the most luxurious. Located in Abu Dhabi's fabulous Emirates Palace, Mezlai was established in 2007. It has outdoor seating, and offers a great wine list *(see p83).*

Brightly lit entrance at Bastakiah Nights

A mouth-watering Lebanese dish at Awtar

Almaz by Momo

Renowned restaurateur Mourad "Momo" Mazouz makes his first foray into Dubai's dining scene with this modish Moroccan establishment. Snack on mezze or enjoy Moroccan classics such as pigeon pastilla before checking out their sheesha salon. ✆ Map C2 • Mall of the Emirates • 04 409 8877 • Open 10am–midnight Sun-Thu, 10am–1:30am Fri, 10am–midnight Sat • No alcohol • DDD

Bastakiah Nights

With its rooftop overlooking historic Al Fahidi, this is a gem of a restaurant offering unrivalled views of old Dubai. A must-visit for authentic Arabic and Emirati cuisine, seated at a low table overlooking the torch-lit court-yard or in an intimate indoor room (see pp12–13).

Pars Iranian Kitchen

Widely viewed as the best inexpensive Iranian restaurant in the city, this branch, located next to the Rydges Hotel in Satwa (there's another branch inside the Mall of the Emirates) is the most popular. Traditional fare includes kebabs and a mixed grill of chicken and lamb with rice. You can sit alfresco or eat indoors. ✆ Map E4 • Al Dhiyafa St • 04 398 4000 • Open 6:30pm–1am daily • No alcohol • DD

Top 10 Restaurants

1 Table 9
A fine-dining experience in an upmarket setting (see p63).

2 Mezzanine
Visit for British classics, once overseen by celebrity chef Gary Rhodes. ✆ Map B2 • Grosvenor House Dubai, Dubai Marina • 04 399 8888 • Open 7–11:30pm • DDDDD

3 EauZone
Poolside setting and imaginative fusion cuisine. ✆ Map B2 • One&Only Royal Mirage, Al Sufouh • 04 399 9999 • Open noon–1am • DDDDD

4 Fire & Ice
Contemporary culinary fireworks and icy concoctions (see p71).

5 Zuma
Fashionable Japanese; sit at the sushi bar or at the comfy tables. ✆ Map D5 • DIFC, Sheikh Zayed Rd • 04 425 5660 • 12:30–3pm, 7pm–midnight • DDDD

6 Reflets par Pierre Gagnaire
Located in the Inter-Continental Dubai Festival City hotel, the superb Reflets restaurant offers fine dining from the French master Pierre Gagnaire (see p63).

7 Bord Eau
French classics and contemporary dishes at this chic restaurant (see p93).

8 Hoi An
French-Vietnamese fusion cuisine served in a Far-Eastern atmosphere (see p76).

9 Zheng He's
Superb Chinese delicacies served in style at an exquisite waterside location. The dim sum is delicious (see p83).

10 Peppercrab
Sensational upmarket oriental seafood (see p71).

For a guide to restaurant prices, see p63.

Left **The stylish Bar 44** Centre **Sho Cho's wooden deck** Right **Moroccan-styled The Rooftop**

Best Bars in Dubai

The Rooftop

It's easy to fall in love with the magical look and feel of this atmospheric Moroccan-style rooftop bar with its Arabesque lanterns and Oriental lounge music *(see p85)*.

Bahri Bar

You'll be impressed with the enchanting old-Arabian architecture and sumptuous interiors of Mina A'Salam hotel and its colonial-styled bar with verandas covered in Persian carpets. It also offers a mesmerizing view of the Burj Al Arab *(see p85)*.

Sho Cho's

There is no more sublime spot for a drink than on Sho Cho's wooden deck by the beach. Low-key early in the evening when people come for the sushi, Dubai's style-setters pack the place late for excellent DJs *(see p85)*.

Nasimi Beach

A stunning beachfront spot for an evening drink with the backdrop of the Dubai skyline and resident international DJs doing their thing. Friday nights are the most lively, but any night is enjoyable to relax on a bean bag cushion with a drink. ⚙ *Map B2 • Atlantis, Palm Jumeirah • 04 426 2626 • Open noon–1am*

Buddha Bar

You'll want to linger at this atmospheric bar, which attracts a fashionable crowd of regulars

Plush interior of 1897

who flock here for the Oriental decor, Asian tapas and exotic cocktails. This one is better than its more touristy Paris parent. Expect to see some dancing on the tables *(see p85)*.

1897

This stylish cocktail bar is named after the year Kempinski Hotels were founded. Sink into a purple velvet sofa and enjoy some of the best cocktails in Dubai, along with smooth jazz sounds. ⚙ *Map C2 • Kempinski Mall of the Emirates Hotel, Dubai • 04 341 0000 • Open noon–2am*

Neos

On the 63rd floor of The Address Hotel, Neos offers unbeatable views across central Dubai – the only building taller than the hotel is the nearby Burj Khalifa. Sit back and relax into the Art Deco furniture and watch the impressive Dubai Fountain. ⚙ *Map C6 • Address Hotel, Emaar Blvd, Dubai • 04 436 8888 • Open 6pm–2:30am*

 Dubai's resident expats hit the city's bars around 6pm for sunset or after 10pm for post-dinner drinks.

The Terrace

Reclining on one of the low sofas listening to the water lapping at the boats on Dubai Creek is about as relaxing as it can get. Add some oysters, champagne and caviar (the house specialities) to the equation and you're bound to have a sublime experience. Vodka lovers will be pleased – the Terrace prides itself on its extensive vodka menu (see p65).

Bar 44

Prop yourself up at the swanky circular bar or sink into a plush chair at this swish cocktail bar on level 44 (hence the name) of the Grosvenor House hotel with spectacular views over Dubai Marina. It attracts a regular sophisticated local set as well as visiting businesspeople out to impress colleagues (see p85).

Left Bank

Sat snugly within the Arabic-themed maze of Souk Al Bahar, Left Bank is the discerning choice for Dubai expats looking for a little bit of sophistication and privacy. The bar is dimly lit and exquisitely decorated and provides the perfect spot for a cosy drink or a bite to eat. ⓢ Map B6 • Souk Al Bahar, Sheikh Zayed Rd • 04 368 4501 • Open 6pm–2am daily

Colonial-style interior of the Bahri Bar

Top 10 Sheesha Spots

The Courtyard

Relax in a shady cushion-strewn courtyard. ⓢ Map B2 • One&Only Royal Mirage Hotel, Jumeirah, Dubai • 04 399 9999 • Open 7pm–1am

Kan Zaman

A smoke under the stars. ⓢ Map K1 • Heritage & Diving Village, Shindagha, Dubai • 04 393 9913 • Open 11pm–3am

Shimmers

A deluxe wooden beach shack with views of the Burj al Arab. Mina A'Salam Hotel (see pp16–19).

Shakespeare's

Popular French Baroque–style patisserie. ⓢ Map D4 • The Village Mall, Jumeirah Beach Rd, Jumeirah, Dubai • 04 344 6228 • Open 8am–1am

Souq Madinat Jumeirah Plaza

A breezy, magical sheesha-smoking spot (see pp18–19).

QDs

An expat favourite overlooking the Creek (see p65).

Barouk

Lebanese dinner spot with traditional entertainment and sheesha terrace. ⓢ Crowne Plaza, Yas Island, Abu Dhabi

Al Areesh

A palm-frond summer house on the waterfront. ⓢ Map K1 • Heritage & Diving Village, Shindagha, Dubai, and the Mina (port), Abu Dhabi • 04 324 3000 • Open 5pm–1am

Al Hakawati Café

Smoke amongst towering skyscrapers. ⓢ Map B2 • Dubai Marina, Jumeirah, Dubai • 04 343 3128 • Open 10am–1am

Special Sheesha Café

Join the locals at these simple cafés. ⓢ Branches on Abu Dhabi Corniche • Open 24 hours

Smoking flavoured tobacco from a sheesha pipe, also known as a hubbly bubbly or hookah pipe, is a popular Emirati pastime.

Left **The Jumeirah Beach Hotel** Centre **Mina A'Salam's beach** Right **Pool at Mina Seyahi Resort**

Beach Resorts

One&Only Royal Mirage
This luxury resort oozes old-fashioned Moroccan romance. Built in truly regal style, it sits on its own sandy beach, amidst acres of landscaped gardens filled with beautiful palm-fringed pools, gushing fountains and candlelit walkways. Explore this divine escape's three intimate properties: The Palace, the Arabian Court and the Residence & Spa. ✆ *Map B1 • Al Sufouh Rd, Jumeirah, Dubai • 04 399 9999 • www.oneandonlyresorts.com • DDDDD*

Mina A'Salam
For a room with a view, this magical kasbah-inspired hotel, part of the vast Arabian-style Madinat Jumeirah, will not disappoint. It is built overlooking an enchanting harbour around which much of the hotel experience is based. Relax in your room's sea-facing balcony, which opens onto the soft sand beach or chill on the extensive terraces of its many restaurants, bars and lounges *(see pp18–19)*.

A beach pavilion at One&Only Royal Mirage

Al Qasr
Designed in the style of a mythical Arabian palace, this magnificent hotel has deluxe rooms and suites. Surrounded by water, it forms a virtual island that offers you a view of ancient windtowers, pools, meandering waterways and the pristine white sand beach *(see pp18–19)*.

Jumeirah Beach Hotel
Set on the shores of the Arabian Gulf and built in a startling shape that mirrors a breaking wave, this landmark 600-room hotel has its own beach and six swimming pools. If you are feeling adventurous, try the adjacent Wild Wadi Water Park, to which guests have unlimited access. ✆ *Map C1 • Jumeirah Rd, Jumeirah, Dubai • 04 348 0000 • www.jumeirahbeach hotel.com • DDDDD*

Atlantis, The Palm
Atlantis opened with a firework display bigger than that of the Beijing Olympic Games. A giant castle at the end of the Palm Jumeirah, this enormous resort boasts a fantastic water-park, an aquarium, a dolphin habitat and several kilometres of private beach. ✆ *Map B1 • The Palm Jumeirah, Dubai • 04 426 0000 • www. atlantisthepalm.com • DDDD*

Le Meridien Mina Seyahi Beach Resort
If you love outdoor pursuits, this relaxed resort is just right for

 For price categories, see p63.

The impressive Atlantis on The Palm Jumeirah, Dubai

you. Indulge in a variety of activities, including tennis, sailing, wind-surfing and deep-sea fishing. ✪ *Map B1* • *Al Sufouh Rd, Jumeirah, Dubai* • *04 399 3333* • *www. lemeridien-minaseyahi.com* • *DDDDD*

Ritz Carlton

With Mediterranean architecture, tropical gardens leading to a golden beach and just 138 guest rooms, this hotel promises exclusivity. Especially good for couples with made-for-two sun loungers, an adults-only pool, a Balinese spa and classy sunset bars and restaurants. ✪ *Map B1* • *Al Sufouh Rd, Jumeirah, Dubai* • *04 399 4000* • *www.ritzcarlton. com* • *DDDDD*

Hilton Dubai Jumeirah

If it's a beach holiday you are after, this 400-room family-focused resort offers comfortable rooms with balconies, a white sandy beach

and a massive pool with a swim-up bar. Try the in-house restaurant, BiCE *(see p83)*, for some fine Italian food. ✪ *Map B1* • *Al Sufouh Rd, Jumeirah, Dubai* • *04 399 1111* • *www.hilton.com* • *DDDDD*

Habtoor Grand Resort & Spa

This shiny 446-room modern resort is located on the seafront, close to Dubai Marina. Guest rooms are located within two high towers, all with garden or sea views. The hotel has its own private beach, three swimming pools, a spa, a health club, restaurants, squash and tennis courts, a children's club and a beach water sports centre. Make sure you visit the stunning infinity pool on the mezzanine between the towers. ✪ *Map B1* • *Al Sufouh Rd, Jumeirah, Dubai* • *04 399 5000* • *www.grandjumeirah. habtoorhotels.com* • *DDDDD*

Westin Mina Seyahi

Aside from boasting Westin's usual elegance and an impressive array of bars and restaurants, the Mina Seyahi has become a top centre for watersports. Should you tire of the pristine private beach and swimming pools, you can sign up for wakeboarding, windsurfing or even charter your own yacht. ✪ *Map B1* • *Al Sufouh Rd, Jumeirah, Dubai* • *04 399 4141* • *www. westinminaseyahi.com* • *DDDD*

Left **The ESPA Spa** Right **Senso, Wellness Centre**

TOP 10 Spas

1 Assawan Spa

The infinity pool in this stunning spa with its lavish ancient Middle Eastern decor, 18 floors up above the Arabian Gulf, says it all: pure luxury, with its long views of sea and sky. Visit for exotic massages and wraps *(see pp16–17)*.

2 ESPA Spa

A Moroccan hammam with heated marble tables under soaring domes is a signature feature of this understated spa. It has 12 luxury treatment rooms. ⊗ *Map B2 • One&Only Royal Mirage, Dubai • 04 399 9999 • www.oneandonlyresort.com*

3 Talise Spa

Arrive by abra along waterways to the 26 treatment rooms, including sunken, wet, colour, crystal and light therapy rooms. There is a 25-minute consultation session before the treatment – the choice here is extensive. ⊗ *Map C2 • Madinat Jumeirah, Dubai • 04 366 6818 • www.madinatjumeirah.com*

4 Softouch Spa

This spa uses Ayurvedic healing combined with a range of modern techniques to combat the stress and strain of modern lifestyles. ⊗ *Map C2 • Kempinski Mall of the Emirates Hotel • 04 409 5909 • www.softouchspa.com*

An objet d'art at the Softouch Spa

5 Spa at Fairmont Dubai

This is a Greco-Roman themed spa with terrace sun-decks and a unique Middle Eastern feel to the treatments. ⊗ *Map E5 • Fairmont Hotel, Sheikh Zayed Rd, Dubai • 04 331 8800 • www.fairmont.com*

6 Cleopatra's Spa

The spirit of ancient Egypt infuses this spa. Some original treatments include O-Lys light therapy and exotic lime and ginger exfoliation. ⊗ *Map H5 • Wafi City, Dubai • 04 324 7700 • www.waficity.com*

7 Urban Male Lounge

A full-service male spa that offers signature facials and massages designed just for men. The "executive" packages are good value, including everything from haircuts to shoe shining. ⊗ *Map 6D • DIFC • 04 425 0350 • www.nstyleintl.com*

The serene decor at Spa at Fairmont Dubai

 For a luxurious day of pampering, be sure to phone ahead and reserve a place. Ask if any promotional packages are available.

Egyptian-themed Cleopatra's Spa

Top 10 Spa Treatments

1 Canyon Love Stone Therapy
A 75-minute massage using warm and cold volcanic stones. ❧ *ESPA Spa*

2 Frangipani Body Nourish Wrap
Tahitian coconut and frangipani flowers are used to give a glow. ❧ *Cleopatra's Spa*

3 Caviar Body Treatment
A whole-body massage using La Prairie caviar-based products. ❧ *Assawan*

4 Sleepy Time
Especially effective after a long journey, this calming massage uses excellent relaxation oils. ❧ *Talise Spa*

5 Ayurveda Massage
A head-to-toe massage by two therapists using synchronous rhythm. ❧ *Softouch Spa*

6 Essence of Moroccan Rose Oil
Exfoliation followed by a Moroccan rose oil massage. ❧ *Spa at Fairmont Dubai*

7 Body Mask
An anti-aging massage and body mask using Ingrid Millet products. ❧ *Senso*

8 Blueberry and Blackberry Facial
A delicious cocktail of natural fruit extracts to hydrate and rejuvenate. ❧ *Hiltonia Spa*

9 Sea Tonic Firming Treatment, Eden Spa
A revitalising body massage and facial treatment using French-derived phytomer. ❧ *Eden Spa*

10 Placenta Diamond Facial
A-list favourite that uses extract of human placenta to oxygenate the skin. ❧ *Biolite Skin Clinic*

Senso, Wellness Centre
8 A contemporary urban spa located in the heart of Dubai Media City with five differently themed treatment rooms. Choose from a vast selection of therapies guaranteed to chase the stress away. ❧ *Map B2 • The Radisson Blu Hotel, Dubai Media City, Dubai • 04 366 9111 • www.radissonblu.com*

Eden Spa & Health Club
9 Soothing daylight and the sound of rippling water create an air of serenity here. The "aqua-medic" pools are filled with mineral-rich waters and situated under a glass-domed ceiling. Treatments include massage, aromatherapy, wraps and mineral baths. There's also a Turkish hammam here. ❧ *Map P1 • Le Meridien, Abu Dhabi • 02 644 6666*

Hiltonia Spa
10 There are five treatment rooms at this very professionally managed spa. Spa users can enjoy the eucalyptus steam room, cold plunge shower, sauna and whirlpool overlooking the resort's own beach and swimming pools. ❧ *Map P6 • Hilton Hotel, Abu Dhabi • 02 692 4205*

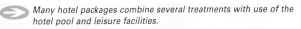

Many hotel packages combine several treatments with use of the hotel pool and leisure facilities.

Left **Lift stop at Ski Dubai** Centre **Encounter Zone at Wafi Mall** Right **Jungle ride, Sega Republic**

🔟 Activities for Kids

Wild Wadi Water Park
Dare to try the 30 adrenaline-fuelled watery rides or just float about on a rubber ring along the waterways here *(see pp78–81)*.

Ski Dubai Snow Park
Go skiing or snowboarding on the slopes of this icy dome *(see p32)*. ⊗ *Map C2 • Mall of the Emirates, Dubai • 04 409 4000 • Open 10am–11pm Sun–Wed, 10am–midnight Thu–Sat • Adm • www.skidxb.com*

Dubai Museum
The clever reconstructions will ensure that you enjoy the experience of an Arabian souq's aroma of spices or the sounds of an old school *(see pp8–9)*.

Stargate
Kids will love the 3D games, space maze, 3D theatre and IMAX cinema. ⊗ *Map F6 • Za'abeel Park, Dubai • 04 800 9977 • Adm*

Aquaventure
Sprawled across 17 ha (43 acres) next to the Atlantis resort on the Palm Jumeirah, this vast waterpark has plenty to thrill visitors. Travel through rapids, waterfalls and the death-defying Leap of Faith slide. ⊗ *Map B1 • Palm Jumeirah, Dubai • 04 426 0000 • www.atlantisthepalm.com*

Magic Planet
There's everything from a merry-go-round, bumper cars, pitch and putt and video games for children to a soft-play area for toddlers, to ensure that you can shop in peace! ⊗ *Map L5 • Deira City Centre (see p62) • 04 295 4333 • Adm for rides • www.deiracitycentre.com*

Sega Republic
Inside The Dubai Mall sits this enormous amusement arcade and theme park. The latest games, plus a whole host

The Wild Wadi's water delights

 The admission fee for Ski Dubai Snow Park includes hire of all the necessary equipment for children.

The fun-filled Za'abeel Park

of rides make Sega Republic
a firm favourite with local kids.
◆ Map C6 • The Dubai Mall, Dubai • 04
448 8484 • www.segarepublic.com

Jumana, Secret of the Desert

The longest running show in Dubai
is held in the Al Sahra Desert
Resort's amphitheatre. Jumana
features stunning pyrotechnics
and aqua and laser effects, as
well as dancing and acrobatics.
◆ Al Sahra Desert Resort, Dubai
• 04 367 9500 • www.alsahra.com

Dubai Desert Extreme Skate Park

Adventurous kids will love the
half-pipes, trick boxes, rail slides
and mini-ramps for BMX-ers,
skateboarders and inline skaters.
All equipment can be hired;
helmets are compulsory. ◆ Map
J6 • Creekside Park, Dubai • 04 336 7633
• Open 2–10pm Sat–Wed, noon–11pm
Thu–Fri • Adm

Encounter Zone

Another shop and drop
deal for kids. Lunarland is for
under-8s, with a snow capsule,
gentle rollercoaster and Skylab
tunnels. Older kids can try the
Galactica's Crystal Maze (a
challenging mental game), the
anti-gravity racing simulator and
3D cinema. ◆ Map H5 • Wafi
Shopping Mall, Dubai • 04 324 7747
• Open 10am–10pm Sat–Wed, 10am–
midnight Thu–Fri • Adm

Top 10 Parks, Gardens & Beaches

1 Creekside Park
A huge botanical park with
BBQ areas, mini golf course
and cable car (see pp10–11).

2 Za'abeel Park
Technology-themed park
with football field, boating
lake and cafés (see pp72–75).

3 Al Seef Rd Park
A great place to enjoy the
Creek action. ◆ Map K2 • Dubai

4 Jumeirah Beach Park
Landscaped play areas
and a beach with showers and
sunbeds (see pp78–81).

5 Al Mamzar Beach Park
Enjoy the huge picnic
areas and four swimming
beaches by hired bike or the
park mini train. ◆ Map F1
• Al Hamriya, Dubai • 04 296
6201 • Open 8am–10pm
• Adm • Mon is for women
and children (boys under 4) only

6 Umm Suqeim Beach
Public beach with shallow
waters and great views of the
Burj Al Arab. ◆ Map C2 • Off
Jumeirah Beach Road, Dubai

7 Safa Park
A huge park with lots to
do. Try the trampoline cage
for fun (see pp78–81).

8 Mushrif Park
A desert park with pools,
an enclosure with farm
animals and a miniature
house exhibit. ◆ Dubai • Open
8am–10:30pm Sat–Wed, 8am–
11:30pm Thu–Fri • Adm

9 Russian Beach
This lively local beach is
popular with Russian expats
and tourists. ◆ Map D4

10 Kite Beach
Popular for kite surfing
and parasailing. ◆ Map C2
• Umm Suqeim, behind
Wollongong University, Dubai

Left **Wind surfing** Right **Pro-karts at the Dubai Autodrome**

Outdoor Activities

Scuba Diving

A popular local activity, you will find good diving in Dubai, Abu Dhabi and some of the East Coast towns. ◈ *Map K1 • Emirates Diving Association, Heritage and Diving Villages, Shindagha, has information on diving in the UAE • 04 393 9390 • www.emiratesdiving.com*

Fishing

Join an organized fishing trip where equipment is provided. Cook your fish on board or even charter your own boat. ◈ *Map B2 & Q1 • Le Meridien Mina Seyahi Resort, Dubai (see p44); Marina Beach Rotana Hotel & Towers, Abu Dhabi (see p116)*

Kite Surfing

Join the friendly local kite surfers on Dubai's popular Kite Beach. You can hire or buy equipment from North Kites, who can help connect you with instructors. ◈ *Map C1 • Kite Beach, Jumeirah Rd, Jumeirah Beach, Dubai • UAE Kitesurfing: www.ad-kitesurfing. net; North Kites: 04 394 1258, www.northkites.com*

Wind Surfing

Great winds make Dubai ideal for wind surfing. Most good beach resorts hire out wind-surfing equipment and also offer wind surfing lessons. ◈ *Map B1 • Westin Mina Seyahi (see p45)*

Sailing

The Gulf winds are great for sailing. Hire a catamaran if you are an experienced sailor.

Beginners can take lessons. ◈ *Map B2 • Le Meridien Mina Seyahi Resort & Marina, Dubai (see p44); Abu Dhabi International Sailing School, Abu Dhabi Marina: 02 681 3446*

Golfing

Both Dubai and Abu Dhabi are awash with world-beating courses, and new ones appear to spring up each month. Several international competitions take place every year, including the Dubai Desert Classic at the city's largest course, the Emirates Golf Club. ◈ *www.dubaigolf.com*

Hot-air Ballooning

Getting a bird's-eye-view from a hot-air balloon is simply sublime. Only by floating way above the dunes can you fully appreciate the waves of sand and patterns of light and shadow

A hot-air balloon set to take off

A wakeboarder in action

crafted by the ridges that are impossible to see from the ground. 🔍 *Dubai • 04 285 4949 • Oct–May • www.ballooning.ae*

Wakeboarding

Try your hand at some wakeboarding tricks as you ride the waves on the Arabian Gulf sea. Ask your resort for a trainer if you're a first-timer. 🔍 *Map B2 & P6 • Le Meridien Mina Seyahi Resort & Marina, Dubai (see p44); Hiltonia Beach Club, Abu Dhabi: 02 692 4205, www3.hilton.com*

Horseriding

Where better to mount a horse than in the Middle East's undisputed equestrian capital? Indulge in a bit of horseriding in Dubai or even a polo match in Abu Dhabi. 🔍 *Map D3 • Emirates Equestrian Centre, 050 558 7656; Abu Dhabi Equestrian Club, Al Ain, 02 445 5500*

Motor Racing

Adrenaline-junkies can burn rubber driving pro-karts at the Dubai Autodrome. The Formula 1 standard racing circuit has 17 hair-raising turns! Book ahead for lessons at the driving school. 🔍 *Dubai Autodrome Kart-drome, Emirates Rd, Dubai • 04 367 8700 • www.dubaiautodrome.com*

Top 10 Golf Courses

Emirates Golf Club
The famous Dubai Desert Classic is held here *(see p53)*. 🔍 *Map B2 • 04 380 2222 • www.dubaigolf.com*

The Montgomerie
A splendid course with sprawling, undulating lawns. 🔍 *Map B2 • 04 390 5600 • www.themontgomerie.com*

Dubai Creek Golf & Yacht Club
One of the world's best, by the Creekside *(see pp58–61)*.

The Desert Course
Challenging lush fairways through desert sands. 🔍 *Map B3 • 04 366 3000 • www.arabianranchesgolf dubai.com*

Yas Links Abu Dhabi
Stunning coastal views with Andalucian-style clubhouse. 🔍 *www.yaslinks.com*

The Els Club
18-hole, par-72 club course. 🔍 *Map B2 • Sports City • www.elsclubdubai.com*

Al Badia Golf Club
A superb Robert Trent Jones II–designed course. 🔍 *Map E3 • 04 601 0101 • www.albadiagolfclub.ae*

The Resort Course
Enjoy Arabian Gulf vistas as you tee off with the peacocks. 🔍 *04 804 8058 • www.jaresortshotels.com*

Al Ghazal Golf Club
A full-sand course with top-class teaching technology. 🔍 *Near Abu Dhabi International Airport • 02 575 8040*

Abu Dhabi Golf Club
Golfers love this serene 18-hole course. It features on the European Tour list. 🔍 *Map N2 • 02 558 8990 • www.adgolfclub.com*

Left **Dubai Aquarium** Right **The Hyatt Galleria ice rink**

Indoor Activities

Snow Sports
What better place to escape the scorching heat than on the slopes of Ski Dubai. You can have skiing lessons, practice snow-boarding tricks or take the kids on a toboggan ride in the children's snow park *(see p32)*.

Ice-skating
The cities' ice rinks are ideal for cooling off while taking in a bit of local colour. Europeans head to the rinks when they get homesick in winter. *Abu Dhabi Ice-Skating Rink, Abu Dhabi; Off map; 02 444 8458 • Dubai Ice Rink, Dubai Mall; Map C6; 04 448 5111 • Hyatt Galleria, Hyatt Regency Hotel, Dubai; Map L1; 04 209 6550 • Adm*

Movie-going
You're likely to see films from India, the Arab world and the Philippines screening along-side Hollywood blockbusters. *Map C6 & N5 • Reel Cinemas, The Dubai Mall, Dubai; Cinestar Marina Mall, Abu Dhabi • Reel Cinemas: 04 449 1988; VOX Abu Dhabi: 02 681 8484 • Open 11am–late • Adm*

Dubai Aquarium
Take a pause from shopping to marvel at The Dubai Mall's vast aquarium. This impressive underwater world houses 33,000 creatures, including tiger sharks, stingrays and giant groupers. *Map C6 • The Dubai Mall, Dubai • 04 448 5200 • Open 10am–10pm Sun–Wed, 10am–midnight Thu–Sat • Adm • www.thedubaiaquarium.com*

Indoor rock climbing

Rock Climbing
Try your hand at scaling the UAE's only state-of-the-art 15 m (50 ft) high indoor climbing wall. *Map H5 • Pharaoh's Club, Pyramids, Wafi City, Dubai • 04 324 0600 • Adm • www.waficity.com*

Shooting
See how good your aim is in one of ten hi-tech pistol-shooting lanes at the Cinetronic Firearms Simulator Room, or try your hand at clay shooting on outdoor ranges at the Jebel Ali Shooting Club. *Map A2 • Jebel Ali Shooting Club, Jebel Ali, Dubai • 04 883 6555 • Open 1–8:45pm Thu–Tue • Adm*

Bowling
Bowling is a popular pastime amongst Emiratis. There are several bowling alleys dotted around the city, though the lanes of choice in Dubai are at the

Participating in and watching sporting events is a great way to get to know the locals.

Dubai Bowling Centre where there are also arcade games. Expats generally prefer Al Nasr Leisureland. 🔊 *Map A6 & H4*
• *Dubai Bowling Centre, Sheikh Zayed Rd, Dubai; Al Nasr Leisureland, behind American Hospital, Oud Metha, Dubai*
• *Dubai Bowling Centre: 04 339 1010; Leisureland: 04 337 1234* • *Open 9am–midnight* • *Adm; includes shoes*

Ice Hockey
The Abu Dhabi Falcons meet on weekday evenings at the huge Abu Dhabi ice rink and are more than happy for you to join in or cheer them on. 🔊 *Abu Dhabi Ice Rink, off Airport Rd, behind Carrefour*
• *02 444 8458* • *Adm*

Belly Dancing
Join Abu Dhabi's expat women for a lesson or two in how to shimmy like the best of them. 🔊 *Map N1* • *Sheraton Abu Dhabi Resort & Towers, Abu Dhabi (see p116)*
• *Sun & Tue* • *Adm*

Billiards, Snooker & Pool
Hear tales of local life over a friendly game of billiards, snooker or pool. You can also have a game of darts and a lager at an English-style pub. 🔊 *Map P1*
• *Rock Bottom Café, Abu Dhabi (see p96); Champs, Dubai* • *Champs: 04 398 2222* • *Adm*

A game of ice hockey

Top 10 Spectator Sports & Events

1 Dubai World Cup
Dress up for the world's richest horse race with a $6 million prize *(see p35)*.

2 Dubai Desert Classic
Watch the world's best golfers compete in this 4-day tournament *(see p35)*.

3 Dubai Tennis Championships
See the big guns of world tennis serve action at Dubai Tennis Stadium *(see p35)*.

4 Dubai Rugby Sevens
The first leg of the Sevens World Tour, this big excuse for a beer fest is loved by rugby fans the world over. 🔊 *Nov*
• *www.dubairugby7s.com*

5 Camel Racing
Watch Emiratis drive their 4WDs around the track beside their camels. 🔊 *Al Wathba Camel Track, 45 km east of Abu Dhabi* • *Oct–Mar Thu–Fri*

6 F1 Grand Prix
Since 2009, Abu Dhabi has hosted a race at the Yas Marina circuit. 🔊 *www. yasmarinacircuit.com*

7 UAE Football
The fans' choreographed dances and songs are just as riveting as the play on the field. 🔊 *Winter weekday nights*
• *www.proleague.ae*

8 Powerboat Racing
Watch the lightweight catamarans in exciting action. 🔊 *Dec* • *www.f1h2o.com*

9 Dubai Marathon
Runners from all around the world compete on the city streets *(see p35)*.

10 Desert Challenge
Bikes, 4WDs and even trucks take part in this international cross country rally through the desert *(see p35)*.

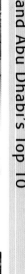

Coincide your visit to the UAE with a major event to see the cities at their best.

Left **Al Ain Palace Museum** Centre **Hatta's Heritage Village** Right **Liwa's sandswept roads**

10 Excursions

1 Sharjah

The Sharjah Art Museum, the Heritage Museum and the Archaeological Museum are a must-visit. The souqs are good for shopping. ◈ *10 km from Dubai*
• *Sharjah Art Museum: 06 568 8222*
• *Heritage Museum: 06 569 3999*
• *Archaeological Museum: 06 566 5466*

2 Al Ain

Known as Garden City, this green emirate is home to the Al Ain Palace Museum. Also here are the Al Ain Livestock Souq and the Jahili Fort. ◈ *160 km from Dubai*
• *Al Ain Palace Museum: 03 751 7755*
• *Jahili Fort: next to Al Ain Rotana Hotel*
• *Al Ain Camel Souq: Al Ain-Buraimi border*

3 Hatta

Visit the Heritage Village at this serene oasis town. A drive into the mountains leads to the clear Hatta Rock Pools. ◈ *105 km from Dubai* • *Heritage Village: Open 8am–7:30pm Sat–Thu, 3–9pm Fri*

4 Fujairah

Fujairah has a coastline of coral reefs and hillsides with forts and watchtowers. The Fujairah Fort is the oldest in the UAE, dating to 1670. Watch a bit of bloodless bull butting on a Friday here. ◈ *130 km from Dubai*

5 Khor Kalba

This small fishing village has the oldest mangrove in Arabia and is now a conservation area. Explore its swamps by canoe.
◈ *10 km south of Fujairah* • *Canoeing: Desert Rangers: www.desertrangers.com*

6 Bidiya

This tiny fishing village is home to the oldest mosque in the UAE, dating back to 1446. Made from mud brick, stone and gypsum, it is now restored with its four small domes held up by a massive central pillar. ◈ *38 km north of Fujairah • Visit outside of prayer times, accompanied by a mosque guide*

The Blue Souq at Sharjah

A *dhow* trip at Musandam Peninsula

Khor Fakkan

A pretty coastal town that sits on a curving bay, this makes a good draw for divers, thanks to the excellent visibility and reef potential. ✆ *15 km north of Fujairah* • *Khor Fakkan Dive Centre: 09 237 0299*

Dibba

A sleepy spot with an open beach. Nearby is Sandy Beach, with one of the best dive centres in the area and close to an ocean outcrop called Snoopy Island – ideal for snorkelling and diving. Sandy Beach Motel is a lovely lunch spot. ✆ *130 km from Dubai* • *Sandy Beach Motel: 09 244 5555* • *Sandy Beach Diving Centre: 09 244 5555*

Musandam Peninsula

Boasting spectacular mountain cliffs and a coastline of inlets and fjords, this northerly enclave is part of Oman. Visit to enjoy day-long *dhow* trips into the fjords, snorkel and see dolphins. ✆ *193 km from Dubai* • *Khasab Travel & Tours: www.khasabtours.com* • *Visa available at Oman entry point*

Liwa

Liwa's high golden dunes, some hundreds of metres high, are almost devoid of vegetation yet close by are flourishing date-producing farms – an awesome spectacle. ✆ *300 km from Abu Dhabi*

Top 10 Tours

1 Arabian Adventures
Enjoy city tours, desert safaris, dune bashing, camel riding, sand skiing and more. ✆ *www.arabian-adventures.com*

2 Net Tours
Reliable city tours, desert safaris, mountain tours, *dhow* cruises plus trips to Oman. ✆ *www.nettoursuae.ae*

3 Bateaux Dubai Cruises
Lunchtime sightseeing and gourmet dinner cruises down Dubai Creek. ✆ *www.jaresortshotels.com*

4 Danat Dubai
Try an Afternoon Sundowner cruise with this *dhow* operator. ✆ *04 351 1117*

5 Creekside Leisure
Recline in a cushioned *majlis* and watch the sun set aboard a *dhow* on the Creek. ✆ *www.tour-dubai.com*

6 Meydan Stable Tour
Visit the world-class racehorse stables and training facilities at the venue for Dubai World Cup *(see p74)*.

7 Arabian Divers & Sportsfishing Charters
Sport fishing in the Arabian Gulf off Abu Dhabi – try to spot dolphins and whales. ✆ *www.fishabudhabi.com*

8 Big Bus Tour Company
Hop aboard an open-air double-decker London bus around Dubai. ✆ *www.bigbustours.com*

9 Wonder Bus Tours
An amphibious 2-hour bus tour that starts on dry land and cruises on Dubai Creek. ✆ *www.wonderbusdubai.net*

10 Orient Tours
Ideal for 4WD tours to Al Ain, Liwa or the Mussandam. ✆ *www.orienttours.ae*

AROUND
TOWN

DUBAI & ABU DHABI'S TOP 10

Left *Dhows* moored at the wharf Right The stunning Dubai Creek Golf & Yacht Club

Around Dubai – Deira

THE TERM DEIRA IS USED TO DESCRIBE *the bustling commercial area north of the Creek. Deira is the source of Dubai's trading roots and it is around the Creek that you really get a sense of this. There is a telling contrast between the sight of the old wooden* dhows *moored at the wharfside reflected in the glass façades of the spectacularly sleek skyscrapers. Much of the* dhow *cargo is destined for the souqs and shopping districts of buzzy Deira. As a result, this area boasts some of Dubai's most atmospheric souq-life, especially at the Gold Souq, Spice Souq and Deira Souq. A major preservation effort by Dubai Municipality means that this area offers some architectural gems like the Al-Ahmadiya School and the Heritage House. The narrow streets and the general traffic congestion in the area mean that to enjoy it all, it's really best to explore on foot.*

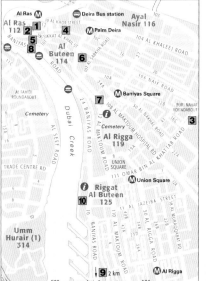

A door at Heritage House

Sights

1	Al-Ahmadiya School
2	Heritage House
3	Watchtower
4	Gold Souq
5	Spice Souq
6	Deira Souq
7	Baniyas Square
8	*Dhow* Wharfs
9	Dubai Creek Golf & Yacht Club
10	National Bank of Dubai

The Al-Ahmadiya School

Al-Ahmadiya School

Dubai's first school, opened in 1912, was founded by a philanthropist pearl merchant. Maths, the Holy Koran and Arabic calligraphy were taught. The boys sat on palm mats. Many such schools were located in Emirati coastal cities with the support of leading merchants and Sheikhs, who subsidised the education. This school closed in 1963. Now a museum and worth visiting for its sheer architectural grace, it offers an educational insight into the past. ◎ *Map K1 • Al Khor St • 04 226 0286 • Open 8am–7:30pm Sat–Thu, 2:30–7.30pm Fri*

Heritage House

This beautifully restored airy courtyard house dates back to the 1890s. Unusually, this 10-room building does not have a windtower, but the upper floor is designed with open doors and windows to draw in the Creek breezes. Now a museum giving an insight into Emirati life, you can explore the different rooms, all furnished to period, with dioramas. There are touch-screens too. ◎ *Map K1 • Al Khor St • 04 226 0286 • Open 8am–8:30pm Sat–Thu, 2–8:30pm Fri*

Watchtower

Tucked away in the busy streets of Deira is a surprise: a beautifully restored mud-brick watchtower that stands in its own gardens. This round tower is Burj Nahar. It dates back to 1870 when it was one of three towers that served as part of Dubai's network of defences. Guards would scale the tower and keep watch for invaders during tribal disputes. The short masonry columns projecting above the roof level once held a palm frond *(barasti)* roof. ◎ *Map M2 • Omar Bin Al Khattab Rd*

Gold Souq

You are unlikely to have ever seen so much gleaming gold as in Dubai's historic Gold Souq. The souq is still dominated by Indian and Iranian craftsmen and traders, as it has been for close on a century. It has been restored with a traditional Arabic arcade with arching wooden roof. You'll find jewellery in both Arabic and western styles *(see p20)*.

Gold displays at Deira Gold Souq

 Discover more at www.dk.com

Exotic spices at the Spice Souq

Spice Souq

Moody and atmospheric, the Spice Souq is a sensory trip into the past, where you can wander through a maze of narrow alleyways lined with shops piled high with aromatic spices. You'll find sacks of cinammon sticks, frankincense, cumin, coriander seed and oud. Some great souvenir buys include frankincense (sold with charcoal burner), henna kits (for hand and body decoration), saffron and fragrant rose water (see p20).

Deira Souq

This is where you get a real taste of the melting pot of cultures that is Dubai. This souq is frequented by Emiratis and expats. The shops sell everything from bright Indian clothing to colourful kitchenware to electric household appliances to pirated CDs. It's a fascinating area to wander in. If you do plan to shop, remember, nothing is sold without haggling (see p20).

Deira History

Liberal trade policies are the roots of Deira which, by the early 20th century, had developed the largest souq on the Arabian coast. It became a natural haven for merchants who left Lingah, on the Persian coast, after the introduction of high customs there in 1902. They continued to trade with Lingah, as do many of the dhows in the Creek.

Baniyas Square

This busy commercial square and traffic junction is the heart of Deira's business district and is home to airlines, hotels, restaurants, shwarma stands and businesses. By night, it glows with Tokyo-esque neon lights and signs. The Dubai Department of Tourism and Commerce Marketing has a useful Visitors Information Bureau here. The square is named after the influential Bani Yas tribe of Abu Dhabi, from which the ruling Maktoum family of Dubai is branched. 🖲 Map L2

Dhow Wharfs

A walk along the wharfside besides Baniyas Road allows you to get up close to the painted wooden dhows, the traditional Arabian sailing vessels, moored here. These ships still trade around the Gulf. Their cargo these days is tyres, refrigerators, air conditioners, electronics – just about any modern item! Moored five or six abreast, these dhows have sailed to trade with Dubai from places such as Iran, Pakistan and Sudan since the 1830s. 🖲 Map K3 • Baniyas Rd

Dubai Creek Golf & Yacht Club

This soaring white building, inspired, like the Burj Al Arab, by the sails of a dhow, and sitting amidst rolling greens, is a city landmark, visible from both

Maktoum and Garhoud bridges. Opened in January 1993, the world-class golf course here is the centrepiece of a sprawling leisure complex that also incorporates a 115-berth marina. The separate yacht club incorporates the Aquarium, an excellent seafood restaurant, as well as one of Dubai's most popular alfresco eateries, the Boardwalk *(see p64)*, which sits on stilts and offers a spectacular view of the Creek, especially at night when the illuminated *dhows* pass by. Ⓢ *Map K6 • Garhoud • 04 295 6000*

National Bank of Dubai
Another architectural achievement is the National Bank of Dubai – one of the city's first iconic buildings. Built in the mid-1990s by Carlos Ott, architect of the Opéra de la Bastille in Paris, it is inspired by the *dhow*. Its curved curtain glass wall symbolizes the billowing sail. The base of the building is clad in green glass representing water and its roof is aluminium, the hull of the boat. It is most striking at sunset, when the mirror reflects its gold and silver lights. Ⓢ *Map K3 • Baniyas Rd*

National Bank of Dubai's stunning façade

A Souk Stroll

Afternoon

🕐 Aim to start this walk around 4:30pm, when the souq shops re-open after prayers and temperatures are cooler. Start with an *abra* crossing from the **Bur Dubai Abra Station**. You can disembark at **Deira Old Souq Abra Station** *(see pp10–11)*. Take the underpass beneath **Baniyas Road** to emerge at the **spice souq** entrance. Enjoy a browse among the fragrant alleyways here. Leave the spice souq at **Al-Abra St**, turn right along **Al-Ras St** which leads into **Sikkat Al-Khail St**. Ahead you will see the latticed entrance to the **Gold Souq** with its colonnaded interior *(see p59)*. There are more than 300 jewellery shops to explore (most take credit cards). Wander into the alleyways off the main thoroughfare and enjoy a cup of tea at one of the small cafés. Exit at the gold souq and continue along Sikkat Al-Khail St to the tiny **Perfume Souq**. The shop windows here are a treasure trove of bottles filled with heady Arabian scents, incense and oud.

Evening

🔖 Enjoy an evening snack by continuing along Sikkat Al-Khail St to **Ashwaq Cafeteria**, a down-to-earth café with outdoor tables, serving shwarmas. Next, return to the **Creek** to admire the **Dhow Wharfage**. For a relaxed ending to the day, drop in at Dubai Creek and Yacht Club's **QDs** *(see p65)* and chill with a cocktail and sensational sunset Creek views.

Around Dubai – Deira

Left **Entrance to Al Ghurair Centre** Centre **Textiles at Pride of Kashmir** Right **Paris Gallery's displays**

TOP 10 Malls & Shops

1 Deira City Centre
This lively mall has 340 shops, an 11-screen cinema, a kids' entertainment area and good restaurants. ✪ *Map L5 • Garhoud, Deira • 04 295 1010 • Open 10am–midnight daily • www.deira citycentre.com*

2 Al Ghurair Centre
A mall with an Arabic feel, this is Dubai's oldest. Recently refurbished, with 130 new stores, you can shop for international as well as local brands here. ✪ *Map L3 •. Al Rigga Rd, Deira • 04 205 5309 • Open 10am–10pm Sun–Wed, 10am–midnight Thu, 2pm–midnight Fri • www.alghuraircentre.com*

3 Paris Gallery
Bvlgari, Dior, Chanel – name a perfume and you'll find it at this upmarket store which also has a vast range of cosmetics, sunglasses and jewellery. ✪ *Map L5 • Floor 2, Stand E39, Deira City Centre • 04 295 5550 • www.uae-parisgallery.com*

4 Damas, City Centre
Visit for a choice of branded jewellery and watches, including Faberge, Chaumet and Vacheron Constantin. Mikimoto pearls are a speciality. ✪ *Map L5 • Floor 1, Stand C28, Deira City Centre • 04 295 3848 • www.damasjewel.com*

5 Dubai Festival Centre
A mall with a marina and more than 400 shops and 75 restaurants. ✪ *Map E3 • Al Rebat St • 800 332 22 • 10am–10pm Sun–Wed, 10am–midnight Thu–Sat*

6 Pride of Kashmir
Presented as a mock souq, this store is packed with a wide selection of antique and modern rugs from Iran, Kashmir and Turkey, plus soft furnishings. Pick up a pashmina here, too. ✪ *Map L5 • Floor 1, Stand B9, Deira City Centre • 04 295 0655*

7 Ajmal
Specializing in Arabic perfumes, which are stronger and spicier than Western fragrances, this store will also mix you a signature scent that you can design with the in-house perfumier. ✪ *Map L5 • Floor 1, Stand B24, Deira City Centre • 04 295 3580*

8 Iconic
Find a variety of things at this store: from clothes and gifts to electronics. ✪ *Map L5 • Floor 1, Deira City Centre • 04 294 3444 • www. theiconicstores.com*

9 Sharaf DG
With tax-free shopping in Dubai, electronics can be a good buy. This large retailer stocks everything from cameras and printers to laptops and TVs. ✪ *Map L5 • Floor 2, Deira City Centre • 04 294 8483 • www.sharafdg.com*

10 Virgin Megastore
From western music to souvenir Middle Eastern music, such as traditional *oud*, you'll find what you're looking for here. ✪ *Map L5 • Level 2, Deira City Centre • 04 295 8599 • www.reefmall.com*

 Paris Gallery, Damas, Iconic and Sharaf DG have multiple outlets in the city.

Price Categories

For a three-course meal for one with half a bottle of wine (or equivalent meal), taxes and extra charges.

D	Under AED 25
DD	AED 25–100
DDD	AED 100–150
DDDD	AED 150–250
DDDDD	Over AED 250

Left **Seating at Table 9** Right **The stylish interior at China Club**

🔟 Restaurants

Table 9
Set up by two British expats, this fine-dining destination is a Dubai favourite. Gastronomic surprises are served in a subtle, upmarket setting. ✎ Map K3 • Hilton Dubai Creek, Baniyas St • 04 212 7551 • Open 6:30pm–midnight daily• DDDDD

Aquarium
This restaurant has floor-to-ceiling glass walls and fine seafood on offer. Try the seared scallops with dates. ✎ Map L5 • Dubai Creek Golf & Yacht Club • 04 295 6000 • Open noon–3pm and 7–11pm • DDDD

The China Club
This elegant restaurant has crisp table linen, striking oriental decor and an extensive menu of dim sum and Chinese classics. ✎ Map K2 • Radisson Blu Hotel • 04 222 7171 • Open 12:30–3pm & 7:30–11pm • DDD

Glasshouse Mediterranean Brasserie
Formerly Gordon Ramsay's, this chic, glass-enclosed casual restaurant serves comfort food classics. Excellent for lunch or an informal dinner. ✎ Map K3 • Hilton Dubai Creek • 04 227 1111 • Open 7am–midnight • DDD

Traiteur
Relish the classic European cuisine as you admire the striking decor. ✎ Map K5 • Park Hyatt Hotel, Dubai Creek Club • 04 317 2222 • Open 6pm–midnight daily & 12:30–4pm Fri • DDDDD

Jamie's italian
Jamie Oliver joined the growing celebrity chef presence in Dubai with this outpost of his wonderful, homely chain. ✎ Map E3 • Festival City • 04 232 9969 • Open noon–midnight Thu & Fri (till 11pm Sat–Wed) • DDDD

The Bombay
This award-winning restaurant is considered to be one of the best curry houses in town. ✎ Map L2 • Marco Polo Hotel, Deira • 04 272 0000 • Open 12:30–3pm & 7:30pm–2am • DDD

Reflets par Pierre Gagnaire
Enjoy fine dining from one of the French masters at the Inter-Continental Festival City hotel. ✎ Map E3 • InterContinental Dubai Festival City • 04 701 1127 • Open 7pm–midnight daily • DDDDD

Blue Flame
An upmarket steakhouse with a thoroughly modern approach to fine-dining. Open kitchens, an oyster bar and a 'cooking school' are also to be found here. ✎ Map L6 • Jumeirah Creekside Hotel, Garhoud • 04 230 8580 • Open 6–11pm Mon–Sat • DDDDD

Blue Elephant
A must-visit for traditional Thai decor, delicious Thai food and a warm Thai welcome. ✎ Map L6 • Al Bustan Rotana Hotel, Al Garhoud Road • 04 282 0000 • Open noon–3:30pm & 7–midnight • DDD

Left **Kiku's minimalist decor** Centre **A noodle dish at YUM!** Right **Fishy dishes at Creekside**

TOP 10 Casual Eateries & Cafés

1 Thai Kitchen
The convenient tasting portions here allow you to sample many Thai delicacies from the four live cooking areas. *Map K5 • Park Hyatt Hotel, near Dubai Creek Golf Club • 04 317 2222 • Open 7pm–midnight • DDD*

2 YUM!
"Live Fast: Eat Fast" is this noodle kitchen's motto. Inspired by different Far Eastern cuisines, it makes for a fun pit stop! *Map L2 • Radisson Blu Hotel • 04 222 7171 • Open noon–11:30pm • DD*

3 Creekside
Savour the freshest of fish, expertly prepared Japanese-style at this elegant restaurant with its teppanyaki station and sushi-sashimi bar and terrace tables with lovely creek-side views. *Map K3 • Sheraton Dubai Creek • 04 207 1750 • Open 7–11pm daily and noon–3pm Sat • DDDD*

4 La Moda
Try some of the great Italian classics with a twist in a stylish setting. The wine list is expansive. *Map L2 • Radisson Blu Hotel • 04 222 7171 • Open 12:30–3:30pm & 7:30–11:30pm • DDDD*

5 Casa Mia
It is "buon appetito" at this homely Italian restaurant, with a rustic decor and fresh breads, pastas and pizzas. *Map L6 • Le Meridien Dubai • 04 702 2455 • Open 12:30–4pm & 7:30–11:30pm • DDDDD*

6 Boardwalk
Built on a wooden veranda over the Creek, with stunning views, especially by night. The menu is varied with light Mediterranean fare and Eastern-inspired dishes. *Map K6 • Dubai Creek Golf & Yacht Club • 04 295 6000 • Open 8am–midnight • DDD*

7 Kiku
Ask to sit in a private tatami room for an intimate Japanese set meal of sushi, teppanyaki, sashimi and tempura. *Map L6 • Le Meridien Dubai • 04 702 2703 • Open 12:30–2:30pm & 6:30–11pm • DDDD*

8 Paul
This bustling French brasserie chain has taken the city by storm over the past few years, serving open sandwiches, salads, and delicious eggs Benedict. *Map L5 • Deira City Centre • 04 295 8404 • Open 8:30am–11:45pm • DDDD*

9 Café Havana
Dig into a light lunch or relax on a couch with a cup of tea, warm scones, sandwiches and pastries. *Map L5 • Deira City Centre • 04 295 5238 • Open 8am–midnight • DD*

10 Automatic
A local Lebanese chain that is a Dubai institution, with fresh food, great prices, friendly staff and branches across the city. *Map L3 • Al Rigga St, Dubai • DD*

Price Categories

For a three-course	
meal for one with half	**D** Under AED 25
a bottle of wine (or	**DD** AED 25–100
equivalent meal), taxes	**DDD** AED 100–150
and extra charges.	**DDDD** AED 150–250
	DDDDD Over AED 250

Left **The terrace at QDs** Right **Dubliners' eye-catching exterior**

Bars, Pubs & Clubs

The Terrace

Made for alfresco drinking and set on the marina front, The Terrace features the Raw Bar, offering a selection of caviar, oysters, prawns and salmon accompanied by an assortment of premium vodkas. ◈ *Map K5 • Park Hyatt Hotel, Dubai Creek Golf Club • 04 317 2222 • Open noon–2am*

Vista Lounge

One of the stylish bars in the InterContinental hotel *(see p114)*, Vista Lounge has stunning views of the Creek and an interesting selection of cocktail creations. ◈ *Map E3 • InterContinental Dubai Festival City, Deira • 04 701 1111*

Eclipse

Cosy cocktail bar with wow factor thanks to its views over Dubai Creek and Sheik Zayed Road. ◈ *Map E3 • Intercontinental Dubai Festival City • 04 701 1111 • Open 6pm–2am daily*

Cu-ba

A swanky rooftop bar that has great views of the creek, and its very own resident DJs. ◈ *Map L6 • Jumeirah Creekside Hotel, Garhoud • 04 230 8459 • Open noon–2am Thu–Fri (till 1am Sat–Wed)*

Irish Village

Throw back a pint or two, along with some fish and chips in Guinness batter, at this Irish-style pub with outdoor bench seating amidst greenery. ◈ *Map L6 • Garhoud, Dubai • 04 282 4750 • Open 11am–1am Fri–Tue & 11am–2am Wed–Thu*

QDs

Lounge at this Creekside wooden-decked terrace bar with a sundowner or chill with a hookah at the *majlis* area while the live band plays. ◈ *Map K6 • Dubai Creek & Yacht Club • 04 295 6000 • Open 5pm–2am*

Dubliners

Another Irish pub that is always packed with expat residents. Inside, it's dark and cosy; outside there's a pleasant patio. A big choice of beers here. ◈ *Map L6 • Le Meridien Hotel, near Airport • 04 702 2508 • Open midday–2am • Happy Hours 5–8pm*

KuBu

Abstract art covers the walls of this late-night nightclub serving a speciality choice of cocktails. The choice of music varies each night according to the DJ but house is big. ◈ *Map L2 • Radisson Blu Hotel • 04 205 7333 • Open 7pm–3am*

Red Square Discotheque

Experience the growing presence of Russia in Dubai, at this buzzing nightspot, located deep in the heart of Deira *(see p63)*.

Belgian Beer Café

A favourite among expats, the BBC, as it is affectionately known, offers a wide range of Belgian ales and dishes. ◈ *Map E3 • Crown Plaza Dubai Festival City • 04 701 1127 • Open noon–3pm, 5pm–2am*

Around Dubai – Bur Dubai

Left **Dubai Museum & Al Fahidi Fort** Right **Sheikh Juma Al-Maktoum House**

Bur Dubai

THIS BUSTLING PART OF THE CITY IS *now packed with hotels, office blocks and residential developments, yet over a century ago it was an area of sand and barasti (palm frond houses) and windtower houses around the Creek. The best spot to get a real sense of old Bur Dubai is the historical Al Fahidi neighbourhood (formerly Al Bastakiya) where the charming courtyard houses have been restored beside the Creek. This lovely atmospheric district is a quiet oasis amidst the city's hustle and bustle. Here too is the imposing Al Fahidi Fort, now Dubai Museum, the original defence outpost for Dubai. The Shindagha heritage area, right at the Creek mouth, is the spot where Dubai's role as an enterprising and cosmopolitan trading city really began. Bur Dubai's souqs, beginning with the textile- and curio-filled old Bur Dubai creekside souq are evidence of this. If you explore the streets further back, into the heart of the dizzyingly-colourful Textile Souq, you'll find a real community feel.*

Bur Dubai Souq

🔟 Sights

1. Dubai Museum & Al Fahidi Fort
2. Al Fahidi
3. Heritage Village & Diving Village
4. Sheikh Saeed Al-Maktoum House
5. Sheikh Juma Al-Maktoum House
6. Sheikh Obaid bin Thani House
7. Bin Zayed Mosque
8. Bait Al Wakeel
9. Bur Dubai Souq
10. Ruler's Court/Diwan

Dubai Museum & Al Fahidi Fort

Once Dubai's main defence outpost, the imposing sand-coloured Al Fahidi Fort was built in 1788 and has also served as a gaol and the ruler's residence. Renovated in 1970, it is now the city museum and worth a visit for an informative overview of the emirate's history. It makes an entertaining visit for all ages: you can walk through a souq from the 1950s, visit an oasis with a *falaj* (irrigation channel), learn about the desert at night and visit a traditional *barasti* (palm frond) house *(see pp8–9)*.

Al Fahidi

This is one of the oldest and most atmospheric heritage areas in Dubai. Here you can wander the alleyways between original, restored courtyard houses, many crowned by *barjeel* (windtowers) which were the earliest forms of air conditioning. Late afternoon is the best time to spend a couple of hours here, when the light throws the architecture into golden relief. The area has become a cultural hub for the city with many buildings converted to art galleries and courtyard cafés *(see pp12–13)*.

Heritage Village & Diving Village

A microcosm of Dubai's cultural and historic past, located near the mouth of the Creek in the old Shindagha conservation area, this traditional complex is a living museum staffed by potters and weavers practising crafts as they have for centuries. There's a tented Bedouin village, armoury displays, handicraft shops, camel rides and an exhibition of Emirati cooking techniques. The Diving Village focuses on Dubai's sea-faring and pearl diving history, with displays of traditional *dhows* and black and white photographs.
🗺 *Map K1 • Al Shindagha • 04 393 7139 • Open 7:30am–10pm*

Sheikh Saeed Al-Maktoum House

Built in 1896 from coral stone covered in lime and sand plaster, this was the home of Dubai's former ruler until his death in 1958. The house was opened as a museum in 1986 and contains collections of photographs, coins, stamps and documents. It's worth visiting for the building itself, with its four windtowers and verandahs. Photographs from the 1950s–80s show seaplanes landing in the Creek and reveal the extraordinary pace of development. Copies of early oil prospecting agreements with international companies make fascinating reading on the Trucial Coast "oil rush".
🗺 *Map J1 • Al Shindagha • 04 393 7139 • Open 7:30am–9pm Sat–Thu, 3–9:30pm Fri • Adm*

A windtower in Al Fahidi

Maktoum family's settlement on Dubai Creek

The Maktoum family's reign as rulers of Dubai began in 1833, when Sheikh Maktoum bin Buti and around 800 tribesmen broke away from the Bani Yas tribe of Abu Dhabi. They settled in Shindagha, an ideal location for trade and for the development of Dubai's pearling and fishing industries.

Sheikh Juma Al-Maktoum House

This building is a superb example of Arab structural design. Built in 1828, the rooms help you learn about the indigenous building materials used – mountain stone, mud, coral stone and gypsum – and the importance of the windtowers for internal cooling. *Map J1 • Al Shindagha • Open 8am–2:30pm Sun–Thu*

Sheikh Obaid bin Thani House

This important property belonged to an influential member of the Qatari royal family who married into the Maktoum clan. A magnificent two-storey house with a courtyard, it was built in 1916. Offset entrances were designed to protect the privacy of the residents. The upper floor has larger openings to draw in the Creek breezes. The large lamp over the entrance harks back to the house's seafaring trading past. *Map K1 • Al Shindagha • Open 9am–2pm Sun–Thu*

Bin Zayed Mosque

An unusual square mosque without a traditional dome, the Bin Zayed Mosque was built in 1968. This spartan little place of worship is still used today. Close by is Al Mulla Mosque, made from mud and topped by a cylindrical minaret – restored according to the oral accounts of elderly Emiratis. *Map J1 • Al Shindagha*

Bait Al Wakeel

A fine example of early 20th-century coral stone architecture, the beautiful Bait Al Wakeel was once the offices of the British East India Shipping Company. This early office building, the first building in Dubai built specifically for administration, is worth a visit to check out the primitive facilities that Dubai's bureaucracy had to contend with. To the rear of the building is a casual eatery offering Creekside views. They offer decent Thai and Arabic

The Ruler's Court/Diwan at dusk

Beautiful street lamps at the Textile Souq

dishes on their menu, and it is well worth taking time out and stopping here for a juice or coffee to enjoy the bustling Creek vistas (see p11).

Bur Dubai Souq

This souq begins at the water's edge by the Dubai Old Souq Abra Station and, since its renovation, is now housed under an imposing arcaded wooden roof. It's a mix of old and new – here you'll find moneychangers, textiles, bargain clothes, glittery Arabian slippers and curios. This souq merges with the Textile Souq, which is fun to explore – here you'll see tailors working on old-fashioned sewing machines (see p21).

Ruler's Court/Diwan

A handsome cream building with imposing windtowers sits beside the Creek next to the Al Fahidi neighbourhood and the Grand Mosque. The striking gold-topped wrought iron gates give a clue to its importance: this is the seat of power and is the Ruler's Court or Diwan, (Persian for couch). This is where Dubai's ruler Sheikh Mohammed's offices are located. ✎ Map K2
• Adjacent to Al Fahidi, Creekside

Around Dubai – Bur Dubai

A Day's Exploration of Old Dubai

Morning

🕙 Start your tour at the **Heritage and Diving Village** at 10am, where you can learn about Emirati crafts and the history of Dubai's pearling industry. Break for fresh lemon and mint juice at any of the nearby waterside restaurants. Now head in the opposite direction to explore the rest of the **Shindagha heritage area**, including a visit to the museum within **Sheikh Saeed Al-Maktoum House** (see pp10–11). Following the curve of the Creek you will arrive at the wooden-arcaded **Bur Dubai Souq**. Enjoy a browse of the textile and curio stalls here. Also, peep down the alleyways for views of restored windtowers and small fabric and tailor shops. At the end of the first covered section of the souq, head left to the Creek for a great view across to **Deira Spice Souq** (see p20). Then wend your way through to **Ali Bin Abi Thalib Rd** – to your right is the unmistakable **Al Fahidi Fort and Dubai Museum** (see pp8–9), where you can easily spend an interesting, informative hour.

Afternoon

Head along **Al-Fahidi St** to the **Al Fahidi** area where you can enjoy a leisurely courtyard lunch inside the restored building of the **Basta Art Café**. Afterwards, spend some time exploring Al Fahidi's alleys and buildings; don't miss **Bastakiah Nights** and the **Majlis Gallery** (see pp12–13).

Left **The atrium at Burjuman** Right **A stained glass Egyptian panel at Wafi City**

Places to Shop

Bur Dubai Souq
This souq starts at the creekside beneath a traditional wooden arcade. Wander through this old renovated souq with small shops and stalls selling a medley of goods from textiles to shoes to bargain clothing to curios *(see pp66–9)*.

Burjuman Mall
This chic shopping mall caters to those with money, with stores selling exclusive labels and glam accessories. ◎ *Map J3 • Trade Centre Rd • 04 352 0222 • Open 10am–midnight*

Lamcy Plaza
A long-established mall where you'll find everyday practical items at very affordable prices – the reason it has remained so popular with expats. The big food court is also a draw. ◎ *Map H4 • Adjacent to Sheikh Rashid Rd–Um Hurair Rd interchange • 04 335 9999 • Open 9am–10pm*

Wafi City
This kitsch, Egyptian-themed, pyramid-shaped building is the place to head if you love fashion. ◎ *Map H5 • Oud Metha Rd • 04 324 4555 • Open 10am–10pm Sat–Wed, 10am–midnight Thu–Fri*

Amzaan
Specializing in funky foreign and Emirati labels, this uber-chic fashionista boutique is a real gem. ◎ *Map H5 • Wafi City • 04 324 6754 • Open 10am–10pm Sun–Thu; 4–10pm Fri*

Wafi Gourmet
Stocked to the ceiling with Arabian cheeses and sweets, barrels of the plumpest olives, dates and truffles, plus boxes of delectable Lebanese pastries and chocolates, it's no surprise that this is Dubai's favourite delicatessen. ◎ *Map H5 • Wafi City • 04 324 4555 • Open 8am–1am*

Computer Plaza
Dubai has often been considered an electronics hub, and this shopping centre, with over 60 specialized retail outlets, is the perfect place to pick up a discounted laptop or digital camera. Software is also available. ◎ *Map H2 • Al-Ain Centre • 04 352 6663 • Open 10am–10pm*

Saks Fifth Avenue
High-end department store that sells designer clothes, perfumes and accessories. ◎ *Map J3 • Burjuman Mall • 04 351 5551 • Open 10am–10pm daily*

Karama "souq"
Hunt for cheap Arabian souvenirs, handicrafts and fake designer goods at this shopping complex. For local flavour, wander around the gritty neighbourhood afterwards *(see pp20–21)*.

Satwa
This suburb is known for its fabrics, tailors and Indian sweet shops – where the local people shop *(see pp20–21)*.

Price Categories

For a three-course meal for one with half a bottle of wine (or equivalent meal), taxes and extra charges.

D	Under AED 25
DD	AED 25–100
DDD	AED 100–150
DDDD	AED 150–250
DDDDD	Over AED 250

Left **An authentic Indian spread at Mumtaz Mahal**

🔟 Restaurants & Cafés

Fire & Ice
This place might resemble a Manhattan-style steakhouse with an identity crisis but there is no crisis of confidence in the kitchen. ✪ *Map H6 • Raffles Dubai • 04 314 9888 • Open 7–11:30pm • DDDDD*

Peppercrab
Devour a tasty, peppery crab at this Singaporean superb seafood restaurant (aprons and pliers provided). ✪ *Map K5 • Grand Hyatt Dubai • 04 317 2222 • Open 7–11:30pm (to 1am Thu & Fri) • DDDDD*

Asha's
Bollywood singing sensation Asha Bhosle's glamorous restaurant has a loyal local following for its Indian classics, daring contemporary creations and equally adventurous cocktail list. ✪ *Map H5 • Pyramids Wafi City • 04 324 4100 • Open noon–3pm & 7:30pm–midnight • DDDDD*

Manhattan Grill
Dig into high-quality juicy steaks at this American diner-styled restaurant. Set menu and vegetarian options are available too. The wine list here is generous. ✪ *Map J6 • Grand Hyatt • 04 317 2222 • Open 12:30–3pm & 7–11:30pm • DDDDD*

Medzo
This stylish Italian-influenced Mediterranean restaurant offers up an imaginative menu in a chic setting. ✪ *Map H5 • Wafi City • 04 324 4100 • Open 12:30–3pm & 7:30–11:30pm • DDDD*

Mumtaz Mahal
Dine here for an intimate Indian meal with traditional live music and authentic cuisine. The *kulfi* desserts are delicious. ✪ *Map K2 • Arabian Courtyard • 04 351 9111 • Open noon–3pm & 7pm–3am • DDDDD*

Kan Zaman
Great Arabic fare in a Creek-side setting in the Shindagha Heritage Area. Watch the water taxis while you enjoy mezze and fresh juices. ✪ *Map K1 • Heritage Village • 04 393 9913 • No alcohol • DD*

Ravis
With its famed butter chicken, Ravis is something of an institution. An inexpensive local favourite, this eatery serves Pakistani cuisine, and keeps the people of the city well fed. The tables are always packed. ✪ *Map E4 • Satwa Roundabout • Open 5pm–3am • No alcohol • DD*

Lemongrass
An innovative and affordable Thai restaurant where you can savour some fresh, authentic dishes. ✪ *Map H4 • Near Lamcy Plaza • 04 334 2325 • Open noon–11:30pm • No alcohol • DDDD*

Basta Art Café
You'll be delighted to have a light lunch or juice at this bougainvillea-clad historic courtyard. ✪ *Map K2 • Al Fahidi • 04 353 5071 • Open 8am–10pm • No alcohol • DD*

Families enjoying the weekend at Za'abeel Park

Sheikh Zayed Road

THE KEY ARTERY OF DUBAI, SHEIKH ZAYED RD *is the outset of the highway direct to Abu Dhabi. It's becoming known as "The Strip" because, just as in Las Vegas, this symbol of Dubai's meteoric development is flanked with the most innovative and contemporary of global architecture. Gleaming skyscrapers tower above the lines of traffic beneath. Symbolically too, the road is the path to the city's future visionary expansion programme. Coming up at Interchange*

One are the Burj Khalifa, the world's tallest building and The Dubai Mall, Dubai's greatest tribute to consumerism. Further out, industrial Al Quoz has become a hub for art galleries.

Burj Khalifa

TOP 10 Sights

1. Za'abeel Park
2. Dubai World Trade Centre
3. Dubai International Financial Centre (The Gate)
4. Burj Khalifa
5. Ras Al Khor Wildlife Sanctuary
6. Souk Al Bahar
7. Al Quoz Art Galleries
8. Meydan Stable & Race Tour
9. The Dubai Mall
10. Emirates Towers & Blvd

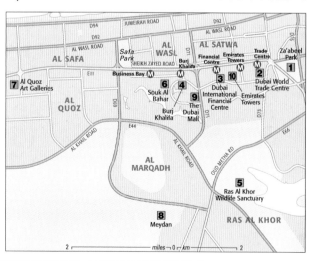

Za'abeel Park

One of Dubai's largest parks, this is a delightful sea of green amidst the city's urban centre and offers spectacular views of the skyscraper-filled skyline of Sheikh Zayed Rd. This beautiful oasis boasts lakes, ponds, a jogging track, cricket pitch, football field, BMX track, play areas, shops and cafés. It is also the Middle East's first "technology park" and has three zones linked by pedestrian bridges: alternative energy, communications and technology, and a space maze based on the planetary system *(see pp48–9)*. Ⓢ *Map F5–F6 • Sheikh Zayed Rd • 04 325 9988 • Open 8am–11pm Sun–Wed, 8am–11:30pm Thu–Sat*

Dubai World Trade Centre

Hard to believe today when you see it dwarfed by the skyscrapers of Sheikh Zayed Rd, but back in 1979 the DWTC was the tallest building in the city, opened with great pomp by Sheikh Rashid and Queen Elizabeth II of England. It has played an important role in the city's development, a fact reflected by the continued use of its image on the AED 100 note. Today, it also comprises 14 huge exhibition halls. The Dubai International Convention Centre next door can accommodate more than 10,000. Ⓢ *Map E5 • Sheikh Zayed Rd • 04 332 1000 • www.dwtc.com*

Dubai International Financial Centre (The Gate)

Behind Emirates Towers is The Gate, the striking 15-storey architectural

Dubai International Financial Centre

signature of the Dubai International Financial Centre (DIFC). This "city within a city" is now a global financial hub with its own civil and commercial laws. The Gate is shaped like a bridge – DIFC is designed to bridge the gap between the financial centres of London and New York in the West and Hong Kong and Tokyo in the East. Ⓢ *Map D6 • Sheikh Zayed Rd • 04 362 2222*

Burj Khalifa

The Burj Dubai, as it was known during its construction, was renamed the Burj Khalifa in 2010 in honour of the President of the UAE. At 818 m (2,700 ft) tall, the tower became the tallest structure in the world long before building work finished. On the 124th floor is an impressive observation deck from where visitors can see just about everything for several miles around. In front of the Burj sits the record-breaking Dubai Fountain, which spurts water some 150 m (500 ft) into the air. Ⓢ *Map C6 • Sheikh Zayed Rd • 04 808 8124*

World Trade Centre

Around Dubai – Sheikh Zayed Rd

Pink flamingos at Ras Al Khor

5 Ras Al Khor Wildlife Sanctuary

Pink flamingos, waders and other birds can be viewed on a marshy reserve at the inner end of Dubai Creek. Managed by the World Wide Fund for Nature and the Emirates Wildlife Sanctuary, this urban reserve has three hides – Flamingo, Mangrove and Lagoon – designed as windtowers, all fitted out with telescopes, binoculars and picture panels. ✆ *Map E2 • Ras Al Khor • 04 606 6822 • Open 9am–4pm Sat–Thu • Free to the hides; groups of more than 10 require permits*

6 Souk Al Bahar

Next to the futuristic Burj Khalifa is a slice of old, albeit newly built, Arabia. Souk Al Bahar is an Arabesque shopping mall with over 100 retail outlets including independent boutiques, souvenir shops and antique stores. Along the souk's waterfront promenade

Godolphin

Probably the most famous racing stable on the planet, Godolphin was established by the equestrian-enthusiast Maktoum Royal Family of Dubai in 1994 and has won Group One races in 11 countries. It bred the great Dubai Millennium, who won the Dubai World Cup 2000 by more than six lengths and sired 59 offspring. ✆ *www.godolphin.com*

there is also a host of eateries, from upscale restaurants to cafés and lounge bars. This is the perfect spot for a stroll before you attempt the shopping madness of The Dubai Mall just a few minutes' walk away. ✆ *Map B6 • Sheikh Zayed Rd • Open 10am–10pm Sat–Thu, 2–10pm Fri*

7 Al Quoz Art Galleries

Al Quoz industrial district boasts the city's most cutting edge contemporary art galleries, including The Third Line, which exhibits provocative art and serious Middle East talent, and Gallery Isabelle van den Eynde, which is quickly developing a reputation for showing important work *(see p34)*.

8 Meydan Stable and Race Club Tour

The tour of this world-class facility includes the chance to see thoroughbred training in action. Take a behind-the-scenes look at the saddling paddock, the jockeys' lounge, the parade ring and the VIP suites that host royals and celebrities. You can choose between the morning tour, which starts with a trackside breakfast, or an afternoon tour, which ends with tea in the grandstand. ✆ *Map D3 • Meydan Racecourse • 04 381 3231 • Open Nov–Apr: Sun, Tue & Wed • Adm • www.meydanhotels.com*

The Dubai Mall

This vast mall has become a premier shopping and entertainment destination. Nearly every mid- and high-end fashion brand can be found here, plus cinemas, games arcades, an aquarium and more to keep visitors entertained. The mall's promenade overlooks the Burj Khalifa and has a range of al fresco restaurants. ◎ *Map C6* • *Next to the Burj Khalifa* • *Open 10am–10pm Sun–Wed, 10am–midnight Thu–Sat* • *www.thedubaimall.com*

Boulevard at Emirates Towers

Two triangular twin towers, clad in aluminium and silver glass, soar into the Sheikh Zayed Road's skyline: the Jumeirah Emirates Towers. The taller is an office block, where Dubai Crown Prince Sheikh Mohammed bin Rashid Al Maktoum has his office, and the other a 400-bedroom luxury hotel joined by a central podium containing a shopping boulevard *(see p36)*. The hotel has a great choice of restaurants and bars. ◎ *Map D6* • *Sheikh Zayed Rd, Dubai* • *04 319 8999*

Jumeirah Emirates Towers

A Shopping, Gallery & Spa Day

Morning

Start your day with some shopping at the swanky **Emirates Towers** shopping boulevard, renowned for its designer stores. Now for some his and her pampering. He should head for **1847**, a classy gents salon, and ask for the 1847 shave – a 35-min old-fashioned treat that includes an oil massage, double shave and mask (Tel 04 330 1847, open 10am–10pm, AED 115, other treatments include facials and pedicures). She should make a beeline for **N.Bar** where she can enjoy the combined manicure & pedicure treatment (Tel 04 330 1001, open 9am–9pm, AED 110). Leave the hotel and drive or take a taxi down the **Sheikh Zayed Rd** to the **Al Quoz** district after interchange no 3 (just before Mercedes-Benz showroom) where you'll find **The Third Line**, Dubai's most important art gallery exhibiting and selling works of art from the region and wider afield. Return to the Sheikh Zayed Rd and continue to the huge **Mall of the Emirates** *(see pp78–81)*. Plenty of choices for lunch here but the **Emporio Armani Caffé** is the most stylish spot *(see p84)*.

Afternoon

Spend the afternoon browsing your favourite shops among more than 400 outlets here at Dubai's biggest retail centre. To rest your feet, catch a movie at the multi-screen cinema. If you are up for a bit of action, cool off with some skiing at **Ski Dubai** *(see pp78–81)*.

Left **Tokyo@thetowers** Centre **Olive House** Right **Spectrum on One**

🔟 Restaurants & Cafés

Around Dubai – Sheikh Zayed Rd

Hoi An
Vietnamese fare served in elegant surroundings with superb cuisine and service. ⊗ *Map C5 • Shangri-la Hotel • 04 405 2703 • www.shangri-la.com • DDDDD*

Marrakech
Live Moroccan folk music accompanies dinner at this atmospheric restaurant. The mezzes and mains are both outstanding here. ⊗ *Map C5 • Shangri-La Hotel • 04 405 2703 • www.shangri-la.com • DDDDD*

Alta Badia
This elegant fine dining restaurant on the 51st floor has food and vistas that are eye-catchingly engaging. ⊗ *Map D6 • Emirates Towers • 04 319 8771 • www.jumeirah.com • DDDDD*

Karma Kafé
Classic Asian fusion food, plush decor and a lovely terrace overlooking the Dubai Fountain. ⊗ *Map C6 • Souk Al Bahar, Downtown Burj Khalifa, Dubai • 04 423 0909 • DDD*

Exchange Grill
This is the best steak restaurant in town – the culinary finesse combines the classic and the innovative. ⊗ *Map E5 • Fairmont Hotel • 04 332 5555 • www.fairmont.com • DDDDD*

Spectrum on One
"Taste a nation" is the motto at this spacious multi-faceted restaurant offering a culturally diverse menu and global cuisine from numerous open kitchens. ⊗ *Map E5 • Fairmont Hotel • 04 311 8316 • www.fairmont.com • DDDD*

Teatro
The cross-Continental dishes here have made this restaurant a firm favourite for many years. ⊗ *Map D5 • Towers Rotana Hotel • 04 343 8000 • www.rotana.com • DDD*

Noodle House
Visit for a quick, affordable and tasty bowl of spicy noodles. ⊗ *Map D6 • Emirates Towers Shopping Boulevard • 04 319 8088 • www. jumeirah.com • DDD*

Tokyo@thetowers
Ultra-modern Japanese – eat on the tatami or at the sushi or teppanyaki bar. ⊗ *Map D6 • Emirates Towers Shopping Boulevard • 04 319 8088 • www.jumeirah.com • DDDDD*

Olive House
Low-priced fresh Lebanese-Mediterranean food make this Beirut-style café ideal for a quick meal. ⊗ *Map C5 • Number One Tower, Sheikh Zayed Rd, Dubai • 04 343 3110 • DD; No alcohol*

Price Categories

For a three-course meal for one with half a bottle of wine (or equivalent meal), taxes and extra charges.

D	Under AED 25
DD	AED 25–100
DDD	AED 100–150
DDDD	AED 150–250
DDDDD	Over AED 250

Left **The Agency bar** Right **The stylish Cin Cin's**

Bars & Clubs

The Agency
Choose from 50 different wines, served in a Manhattan-style ambience. ◈ *Map D6*
• *Emirates Towers Hotel* • *04 319 8088*
• *www.jumeirahemiratestowers.com*

Alta Badia Bar
This sophisticated bar has unbeatable views and a selection of international cocktails. ◈ *Map D6*
• *Emirates Towers Hotel* • *04 319 8771*
• *www.jumeirah.com*

Cin Cin's
This chic champagne bar has a sublime snack menu, featuring freshly-shucked oysters and Wagyu beefburgers. ◈ *Map E5*
• *Fairmont Hotel* • *04 311 8316*
• *www.fairmont.com*

The Act
Unlike the more raunchy original in Las Vegas, this nightspot has been renowned since it opened in 2013. ◈ *Map D5*
• *Shangri-La Hotel* • *052 811 9900*
• *www.theactdubai.com*

Blue Bar
Low-key relaxed bar where you can chill to the tunes of the resident jazz band. ◈ *Map E5*
• *Novotel Hotel, behind World Trade Centre* • *04 332 0000*

Neos
A great spot for gazing down at the Burj Khalifa, the Dubai Fountain and the light show from the 63rd floor of The Address Downtown hotel. Art Deco decor and impeccable cocktails. ◈ *Map C6* • *The Address Downtown, Downtown Burj Khalifa* • *04 436 8927*

Long's Bar
This colonial-style bar, with its small dance floor, claims to have the longest bar in the UAE. ◈ *Map D5* • *Towers Rotana Hotel* • *04 312 2202* • *www.rotana.com*

Harry Ghatto's
This lively Japanese karaoke bar offers over 1,000 songs to sing and great cocktails. ◈ *Map D6* • *Emirates Towers Hotel* • *04 319 8088* • *www.jumeirah.com*

Calabar
With breathtaking views of the Burj Khalifa, this Latin-themed tapas bar makes for a swanky night out with its candlelit outdoor terrace and good drinks service. ◈ *Map C6* • *The Address Downtown, Downtown Burj Khalifa* • *04 436 8922*

Zinc
Always packed, this popular club has an ever-changing line-up of live music and local DJs. ◈ *Map E5* • *Crowne Plaza Hotel* • *04 331 1111* • *www.crowneplaza.com*

Around Dubai – Sheikh Zayed Rd

Left **Public beach** Right **Weekend market at Marina**

Jumeirah & New Dubai

JUMEIRAH, A DISTRICT OCCUPYING THE PRIME BELT *of coastline stretching south-west from the port area, is the most glamorous and hedonistic of the city. It's no surprise that residential property here is pricey – it's the ultimate location for a villa in the sun and the quiet leafy streets are filled with bougainvillea-clad luxury villas, usually with a BMW or a monster four-wheel drive parked outside. Here too are the city's most extravagant resort hotels, including the Burj Al Arab, the wave-shaped Jumeirah Beach Hotel, the Arabian-styled One&Only Royal Mirage and the vast Madinat Jumeirah, plus a string of others stretching out along this all-important coastal strip of the Arabian Gulf. Out at sea is the famous Palm Jumeirah Island, whose villa-topped fronds have extended the coastline by 120km. The area is excellent for shopping and leisure and for enjoying beachlife in general, whether you choose to stretch out on your hotel beach or enjoy any of the public beaches.*

Sights

1. Jumeirah Beach
2. Burj Al Arab
3. Madinat Jumeirah
4. Wild Wadi Water Park
5. Atlantis, The Palm
6. Safa Park
7. Jumeirah Beach Park
8. Ski Dubai
9. Mall of the Emirates
10. Covent Garden Market

The impressive Mall of the Emirates

People soaking up the sun at a beach along Jumeirah

Jumeirah Beach

Strictly speaking, Jumeirah Beach is the 9-km (6 miles) stretch of golden coastline running parallel to the Jumeirah Beach Rd, lined by some of the city's most desirable villa accommodation and hotels. There's a good choice of public beaches at Umm Suqueim, Kite Beach and Russian Beach, while the pleasant Jumeirah Beach Park is a delightful spot to while away a day in the sun. ◎ Map A4 • Jumeirah

Burj Al Arab

Visible from almost anywhere in Jumeirah is the iconic luxury hotel, the Burj Al Arab, a symbol for the city itself and distinguished by its unusual shape mirroring the billowing sail of a *dhow*. Reservations are needed to visit the interior of this opulent hotel. For a great close-up view of the exterior, drop into the Jumeirah Beach Hotel *(see p44)* and take the super-fast glass elevator to the top floor *(see pp16–17)*.

Madinat Jumeirah

This vast leisure and entertainment complex has become a major focus of the Jumeirah area – with its two hotels, Al Qasr and Mina A' Salam *(see pp18–19)* linked by a series of seawater-fed waterways navigated by silent battery-powered *abras*. There are more than 45 restaurants, bars and cafés, many offering waterside views, with the romantic seafood restaurant, Pierchic *(see p83)*, located on a pier that stretches into the Arabian Gulf. Here too you'll find the Madinat Jumeirah Souq, a delightful reconstruction of a traditional Arabian bazaar *(see pp18–19)*.

Wild Wadi Water Park

This huge world-class water park offers a great day out to suit all ages and bravery levels with 31 water-fuelled rides and attractions. Thrill-seekers will not be disappointed by its most challenging ride, the Jumeirah Sceirah – it's the tallest and fastest freefall waterslide outside the US. Well-staffed by lifeguards and with plenty of food outlets, it makes for a fun day out. ◎ Map C1 • Jumeirah Rd • 04 348 4444 • Mar–May & Sep–Oct 10am–7pm; Jun–Aug 10am–8pm; Nov–Feb 10am–6pm • Adm • www.wildwadi.com • There is a cashless payment system using an electronic waterproof wristband

Jumeirah's Beaches and Dubai's Beach Culture

All of the hotels in Jumeirah are fronted by their own private stretches of golden beach onto the Arabian Gulf, but there are plenty of public beaches too, which fill up at weekends. There are also family-friendly beach parks with a small entrance charge: the best in this area is the Jumeirah Beach Park.

Atlantis, The Palm

Opened in 2008 and sitting at the top end of the Palm Jumeirah is the unmistakable Atlantis hotel. This sprawling, aquatic-themed resort boasts a vast beach, an enormous marine park where visitors can swim with dolphins and an impressive adventure waterpark. An extensive range of restaurants and other facilities are also on site to keep the entire family entertained *(see p44)*.

Safa Park

You can't miss the giant Ferris wheel here, offering the best views of this huge land-scaped green park stretching from Al Wasl Rd to Sheikh Zayed Rd. It is hugely popular with local residents, many of whom make the most of its specially-sprung perimeter jogging track. It's great for kids to run free and there's lots of entertainment too with tennis courts, trampolining, mini train, a merry-go-round, obstacle course and lake where rowing boats can be hired. ◈ *Map A5*

Jumeirah Beach Park

This lovely green park, full of mature trees, backs onto a beautiful stretch of white sand beach. It is a real gem and an ideal place to spend a day in the sun, although weekends are best avoided when it gets crowded. You can access the beach from the park along wooden walkways and there is plenty of shade on the sand under the many palm trees. It's great for children and is equipped with lifeguards, a shallow beach, showers, toilets, barbecues, picnic tables and small cafés. ◈ *Map A4*

Ski Dubai

You can't miss Ski Dubai from the Sheikh Zayed Rd, jutting out like a giant space-age tube. Holding over 6,000 tonnes

The green Safa Park

Ski Dubai

of snow, it offers five slopes linked by chairlifts and tow lifts to cater to all ski levels, including the longest black indoor run in the world. There's also a snow park for little ones. Ski gear is provided in the ticket *(see p32)*.

Mall of the Emirates

This is Dubai's swankiest retail complex, with more than 500 shops, selling every product you can possibly dream of. There's also a huge branch of Carrefour supermarket, Harvey Nichols and Debenhams, plus myriad fashion labels. It has a multi-screen cinema and big kids' play area, Magic Planet, plus dozens of cafés and restaurants. ✪ *Map C2*
• *Interchange 4* • *04 409 9000*
• *www.malloftheemirates.com*

Covent Garden Market

Dubai Marina is a stunning marina-side development of luxury apartment towers and offices. Unsurprisingly, alfresco waterside life has really taken off alongside the main pedestrian area, Marina Walk, where there are dozens of outdoor cafés. Friday sees the setting up of Covent Garden Market around the stunning central fountain and dancing water features and the arrival of dozens of colourful stalls selling art and handicrafts. It's a great chance to combine shopping with some sunshine. ✪ *Map B2*

A Day by the Sea

Morning

Start your day with breakfast on the outdoor terrace of **Lime Tree Café** *(see p84)*. Enjoy the gentle morning sun as you sip on some coffee or a juice. Drive or hire a taxi to **Jumeirah Beach Park** where you can take a safe swim. Follow it up with a picnic snack on the manicured lawns. If you want to simply laze about, you can hire a sunbed under the palm trees and spend the morning relaxing in the sunshine. Leave at lunchtime and head to **Madinat Jumeirah** *(see pp18–19)* where you have a huge choice of restaurants at which to enjoy a leisurely late lunch, many overlooking the waterways. Afterwards spend an hour or two shopping for souvenirs or browsing the lovely Arabian-style **Madinat Jumeirah Souq** here.

Evening

Now head to one of Dubai's most atmospheric resort venues, the **One&Only Royal Mirage's Arabian Court**, to the **Rooftop Bar** *(see p85)*. From this alfresco spot, you can sip a cocktail over superb views of **Palm Jumeirah Island** *(see p32)* and watch the sun set over the Gulf. For dinner head to the hotel's **Beach Bar & Grill**, a delightful Arabian-themed seafood restaurant located on decking right on the beach where you can enjoy the sound of the waves. It's worth booking a table here beforehand. The Beach Bar & Grill: One&Only Royal Mirage; 04 399 9999; DDDDD.

Left **Ibn Battuta's exotic interiors** Centre **The Village Mall emblem** Right **Souk Madinat Jumeirah**

ᴛᴏᴘ10 Shopping Centres

Souk Madinat Jumeirah
A reconstruction of a traditional Arabian marketplace within atmospheric Madinat Jumeirah, this magical bazaar offers jewellery, antiques, handicrafts and art, interspersed with bars and restaurants *(see pp18–19)*.

Mall of the Emirates
Prepare to shop until you drop and grab a map when you arrive: you'll need it! This is one of the biggest shopping centres in the region with over 500 outlets and top names including Harvey Nichols, Debenhams and Carrefour *(see p81)*.

Ibn Battuta Mall
Great fun to visit, this themed mall, based on the journeys of Arabian traveller Ibn Battuta, has six shopping zones, food courts and a 21-screen cinema. ✪ *Map A2 • Emirates Hills • 04 362 1900 • www.ibnbattutamall.com*

Mercato Mall
Resembling a vast Italian film set, Mercato is an Italian-themed mall with 90 shops, restaurants and cafés. Good for kids with a fun city play area and an Early Learning Centre. ✪ *Map C4 • Jumeirah Beach Rd • 04 344 4161 • www.mercatoshoppingmall.com*

The Village Mall
An intriguing mix of niche upmarket boutiques fill this pretty shopping centre with its archways, plants and fountains. A good place for finding an exclusive gift. ✪ *Map D4 • Jumeirah Rd • 04 344 0111*

The Walk, JBR
This pedestrian-friendly market offers designer fashion outlets and popular cafés by the beach. ✪ *Map B2*

Dubai Marina Mall
Just when you thought there were enough, along comes another mall. This one has a large selection of fashion boutiques. ✪ *Map B2 • Al Wasl Rd • 04 436 1000 • www.dubaimarinamall.com*

Dubai Mall
With more than 1,200 shops, the Dubai Mall offers the world's largest retail space and an entire family entertainment center. ✪ *Map C6 • Next to the Burji Khalifa • 800 3022 46255 • www.thedubaimall.com*

Times Square Center
This smallish mall features an impressive electronics store. It also has its very own ice lounge where everything, from tables to glasses, is made of ice. ✪ *Map C2 • Sheikh Zayed Rd • 04 341 8020 • www.timessquarecenter.ae*

Jumeirah Centre
This small mall, popular with local residents, has a pleasant coffee shop with outdoor terrace. Sunny Days, a boutique upstairs, sells handicrafts and gifts. ✪ *Map D4 • Jumeirah Rd • 04 349 9702*

Around Dubai – Jumeirah & New Dubai

Price Categories

For a three-course meal for one with half a bottle of wine (or equivalent meal), taxes and extra charges.

D Under AED 25
DD AED 25–100
DDD AED 100–150
DDDD AED 150–250
DDDDD Over AED 250

Left **A table setting at Maya** Right **Indian cuisine with a twist at Nina**

🔟 Restaurants

Tagine
Visit this candlelit restaurant with live music and waiters in traditional dress for a magical Moroccan experience. Its location, from a courtyard within Dubai's most atmospheric Arabian hotel resort, adds to its charm. ◐ *Map B1 • One&Only Royal Mirage, Al Sufouh • 04 399 9999 • www.oneandonlyroyalmirage.com • DDDD*

Maya
Experience new-wave Mexican cuisine within spacious surroundings decorated with Mayan art and modern sculpture. ◐ *Map B1 • Le Royal Meridien Beach Resort & Spa • 04 399 5550 • DDDDD*

Zheng He's
The Chinese cuisine here focuses on fresh seafood. The harbour view is stunning. ◐ *Map C1 • Mina A' Salam, Madinat Jumeirah • 04 366 6730 • DDDDD*

Nina
Sample traditional Indian ingredients with a new twist at this sophisticated restaurant within the lush surroundings of this Arabian resort. ◐ *Map B1 • One&Only Royal Mirage • 04 399 9999 • DDDDD*

Pierchic
Definitely book a terrace table at this seafood restaurant situated on a wooden pier over-looking the Arabian Gulf. ◐ *Map C1 • Al Qasr, Madinat Jumeirah • 04 366 6730 • DDDDD*

Indego
Expect a contemporary take on traditional Indian cuisine at this chic restaurant overseen by Vineet Bhatia, the first Indian chef to be awarded a Michelin star. ◐ *Map B2 • Grosvenor House Hotel, Al Sufouh • 04 399 8888 • DDDDD*

Magnolia
A haven for vegetarians, this upmarket restaurant serves healthy, delicious food in a lovely setting. Ask for a terrace table. ◐ *Map D2 • Al Qasr Hotel, Madinat Jumeirah • 04 366 6730 • DDDD*

Mezlai
The first restaurant dedicated to serving authentic Emirati food in the UAE, Mezlai offers dishes with regal splendour. Try the various lamb dishes, as well as the local fish hammour. ◐ *Map N6 • Emirates Palace, Abu Dhabi • 02 690 7999 • DDDDD*

Butcher Shop & Grill
Dubai's favourite South African steakhouse chain has a branch on The Walk in the marina. Fabulous steaks and alfresco dining are the main draws. ◐ *Map B2 • The Walk, Dubai Marina • 04 428 1375 • DDDD*

BiCE
Art Deco-themed Italian where the seafood, meat, wine menu and live pianist are the draw. A Dubai institution that's busy year-round. ◐ *Map B2 • Hilton Dubai Jumeirah • 04 399 1111 • DDDD*

Left **Fusion food at Fudo** Centre **The popular Lime Tree Café** Right **Visit Finz for seafood**

Cafés & Casual Eats

Almaz by Momo
The creative signature of Mourad Mazouz, founder of Soho London celebrity haunt Momo, is strong in this Moroccan restaurant. ⊗ *Map C2*
• *Mall of the Emirates • 04 409 8877*
• *Open 10am–midnight Sun-Thu, 10am–1:30am, Fri-Sat • DDD; no alcohol*

Emporio Armani Caffé
This is a super-sleek restaurant with classic Italian cuisine prepared by Italian chef Stefano Rutigliano. ⊗ *Map C2 • Mall of the Emirates • 04 341 0591 • DDD; no alcohol*

Toscana
Drop in with the kids for some delicious Italian fare served up in a lovely mock Venetian waterway setting at this family-friendly restaurant. ⊗ *Map C2 • Madinat Jumeirah • 04 366 6730 • DDD*

Bella Donna
Known for its excellent thin pizzas, you'll also find a wide choice of classic pasta dishes at this contemporary styled Italian eatery. ⊗ *Map C4 • Mercato Mall • 04 344 7701 • DD; no alcohol*

Chandelier
This casual Lebanese restaurant next to Dubai Marina's dancing fountain is good for a light lunch or evening meal. It has a pleasant outdoor terrace, where you can also sample sheesha. ⊗ *Map B1 • Dubai Marina • 04 366 3606 • DDD; no alcohol*

Lime Tree Café
This homely café with a shady outdoor garden terrace serves healthy homemade lunches, soups, juices, teas and coffees. The café is popular with the expat crowd. ⊗ *Map D4*
• *Jumeirah Rd • 04 348 8498 • DD; no alcohol*

Maria Bonita's Taco Shop
A visit to Maria Bonita is like being transported to Mexico. This relaxed good-value restaurant serves great tacos, tortillas and salsas. ⊗ *Map C2*
• *Umm Al Sheif St • 04 395 5576 • DD; no alcohol*

Johnny Rockets
This restaurant re-creates the look of a 1950s American diner, serving thick milkshakes and the best burgers in town. ⊗ *Map B2 • Marina Walk (south), Dubai Marina • 04 368 2339 • DDD*

Fudo
Feast on fusion food from Lebanon, Japan, Thailand and Italy, with wonderful fruit cocktails at this off-street patio restaurant with leafy trees. ⊗ *Map C4*
• *Jumeirah Rd, next to Mercato Mall • 04 349 8586 • DD; no alcohol*

Finz
This casual shopping centre eatery offers excellent value Mediterranean cuisine, including lobster ravioli and seafood bisque. ⊗ *Map A2 • Ibn Battuta Mall • 04 368 5620 • DD; no alcohol*

Price Categories

For a three-course meal for one with half a bottle of wine (or equivalent meal), taxes and extra charges.

D Under AED 25
DD AED 25–100
DDD AED 100–150
DDDD AED 150–250
DDDDD Over AED 250

Left **The Rooftop bar** Right **Nasimi Beach**

⭯10 Bars & Clubs

The Rooftop
For a relaxed evening drink under a star-filled sky, this Moroccan-styled bar with its superb views over the Arabian Gulf makes for a memorable experience. ✎ Map B1 • Arabian Court, One&Only Royal Mirage • 04 399 9999 • Open 5pm–1am

Bahri Bar
An ideal spot for a sundowner with its wrapround terrace and views of the light shows of the Burj Al Arab. ✎ Map C2 • Madinat Jumeirah • 04 366 6730 • Open 6pm–2am

Sho Cho's
This super-chic Japanese bar offers a gorgeous terrace overlooking the Gulf and interior walls filled with fish tanks. ✎ Map E4 • Dubai Marine Beach Resort & Spa • 04 346 1111 • Open 7pm–3am

Barasti
One of the city's most popular beach bars, Barasti comes alive on the weekends when revellers sprawl out across the sand. It hosts live music or guest DJs most nights. ✎ Map B1 • Le Meridien Mina Seyahi Beach Resort & Marina • 04 318 1313 • Open noon–3am

Buddha Bar
Expect a chilled-out Asian vibe at this eastern-inspired cocktail bar with its tucked-away alcoves and colossal Buddha centrepiece. ✎ Map B2 • Grosvenor House • 04 399 8888 • Open 8pm–2am

Nasimi Beach
With an outside terrace spilling onto the sand, what better way is there to unwind than sprawled out on a beanbag on the beach with an ice-cold drink? The music is usually good, too. ✎ Map B1 • Atlantis, Palm Jumeirah • 04 426 2626 • Open 9–1am Sun–Thu (till 2am Fri–Sat)

Bar 44
Forty-four different types of champagne are on offer at this top-floor swanky bar with intimate sofas and a giant balcony. ✎ Map B2 • Grosvenor House • 04 399 8888 • Open 6pm–2am

The Agency
This wine bar offers "wine flights" – a chance to choose from 50 different connoisseur-selected wines. ✎ Map D6 • Boulevard, Emirates Towers • 04 319 8088 • Open 9–1am

360 degrees
Located in a glass building perched out at sea at the end of a breakwater, this is ideal for a sunset drink. ✎ Map C1 • Jumeirah Beach Hotel • 04 406 8769 • Open 5pm–2am Sat–Thu, 4pm–2am Fri

Koubba
A rooftop bar of elevated Arabian style offering champagne cocktails. Try the fabulous "espresso martini" for a real wake-up. ✎ Map C2 • Al Qasr, Madinat Jumeirah • 04 366 6730 • Open 6pm–2am

Left **The skyline** Right **Marble domes of Sheikh Zayed Mosque**

Around Abu Dhabi

A STUNNING CITY OF SHINY SKYSCRAPERS LINING *a splendid Corniche, oil-rich Abu Dhabi is the capital of Abu Dhabi Emirate as well as of the UAE. Home to the excellent arts centre, the Abu Dhabi Tourism and Culture Authority, it is also the country's cultural and intellectual capital. It is often compared to New York, with its more glamorous sister Dubai likened to LA. An island-city with plenty of narrow white sand beaches and crystal clear turquoise waters lapping at its shores, Abu Dhabi is popular with beachcombers and lovers of the outdoors. Local residents ritually power-walk along the city's waterfront. The median strips of its wide streets are planted with towering date palms, while its green parks are packed with playground equipment for kids.*

A picnic at a public beach

🔟 Sights

1. Emirates Palace
2. Abu Dhabi Heritage Village
3. Abu Dhabi Corniche
4. Al Markaziyah Gardens
5. Yas Island
6. Women's Handicraft Centre
7. Public Beach
8. Sheikh Zayed Mosque
9. Al Maqtaa Fort & Palace
10. Saadiyat Island

Previous pages **Sheikh Zayed Road, the key artery of Dubai**

The magnificent Emirates Palace

Emirates Palace
Abu Dhabi's magnificent pink palace hotel dominates the western end of the splendid Corniche. The majestic multi-domed exterior is surpassed in extravagance by the dazzling interior, glittering with gold and sparkling with Swarovski crystals. The palace was constructed to provide opulent accommodation fitting for the capital's visiting dignitaries – from Saudi princes to world leaders to Hollywood stars *(see pp22–3)*.

Abu Dhabi Heritage Village
The delightful Heritage Village provides a fascinating insight into what everyday life was like in Abu Dhabi before oil was discovered. A re-creation of a traditional mosque, *barasti* house, Bedouin camp and souq are all worth a look, but the star sight is an intriguing museum set in a fort with fabulous exhibits featuring costumes, jewellery, everyday utensils, pearling tools and weapons. There's an arcade of artisan's workshops where you can watch basket weaving, glass blowing, weaving and brass-beating.
⊗ *Map N5 • The Breakwater, next to the flagpole • 02 681 4455 • Open 9am–5pm Sat–Thu, 3:30–9pm Fri*

Abu Dhabi Corniche
The Corniche curves from one end of the city to the other. Wide enough to accommodate power-walkers, joggers, in-line skaters and cyclists, its paved path is lined with ice-cream dispensers and shady pavilions to escape the heat. ⊗ *Map P5 • Corniche Rd • Open 24 hours*

Al Markaziyah Gardens
In a city of wide, green parks, of which Capitol Gardens, Khalidiya Children's Gardens, Al Mushrif Childrens Gardens and Al Khubeirah Gardens stand out, the Al Markaziyah Gardens is the city's most popular. Head here any time of the day during the cooler winter period, or in the evening during the steamy summer months, and the garden is packed. The parks are open to the public all day. ⊗ *Map P4 • Between 1st St, Al Nasr St, Tariq Bin Zayed St & 26th St • Open 24 hours*

The Corniche

Around Abu Dhabi

Always carry a bottle of water with you when walking around the city, especially during summer.

89

The Discovery of Oil

The Japanese invention of the cultured pearl and the subsequent collapse of the Gulf's pearl industry led to the granting of petroleum concessions by Sheikh Shakhbut bin Sultan Al Nahayan in 1939. It turned out to be a very wise move. The discovery of oil in 1958 and its export from 1962 made Abu Dhabi a very rich city.

Yas Island

Opened in time for Abu Dhabi's inaugural Formula 1 Grand Prix in 2009, Yas Island is an ongoing, multi-billion dollar project that includes far more than just the impressive Yas Marina racetrack. Ferrari World Abu Dhabi, the world's biggest indoor theme park, and Yas Waterworld water park, are dominating features, as will be the Yas Mall, due to open in 2014. The island is set to become one of the region's major tourist attractions. ◈ www.yasisland.ae, www.ferrariworldabudhabi.com

Women's Handicraft Centre

Watch veiled Bedouin women chatting to each other as they demonstrate basket-weaving, embroidery, textile making and henna art in a series of workshops at the rear of the Women's Union. You can also buy their work – which they would greatly appreciate. Browse through the displays of costumes, textiles and jewellery in the Exhibition Hall on your way out. Take your shoes off before entering the workshops and remember not to photograph the women without asking first. ◈ Women's Union, Al Karamah St • 02 447 6645 • Open 7am–3pm Sun–Thu

Public Beach

Join the locals for some sunbathing on the soft white sand or a swim in the crystal clear sea at the public beach at Ras Al Akhdar. Head here early morning for a dip in the warm water, when you might share the sand with horseriders exercising their mounts. The weekends see the city's workers here for games of cricket. It is advisable to dress modestly until you're on the beach itself. ◈ Map N6 • Ras Al Akhdar, past the Diwan, Corniche Rd West

Sheikh Zayed Mosque

This impressive structure is the eighth largest mosque in the world and a striking sight on the drive from Dubai to Abu Dhabi. The mosque is named after Sheikh Zayed bin Sultan Al Nahyan, the founder and the first President of the United Arab Emirates, who is also buried here. The building can accommodate 40,000 worshippers, although tours are available to non-Muslims. Visitors should dress conservatively, wearing loose-fitting clothing that covers the arms and legs. This applies to both men and women, and women should also wear a

Weaving at the Women's Handicraft Centre

Al Maqtaa Fort & Palace

headscarf. Shoes must be removed before entering the mosque. ✎ *Al Khaleej Al Arabi St • 02 800 555 • Open 9am–10pm Sat–Thu, 4:30–10pm Fri (tours at 9am & 10am Sun–Thu)*

Al Maqtaa Fort & Palace

This splendid 200-year old sand-coloured fort has intricately carved wooden doors and shut-tered windows. It has one white watchtower on a tiny island in the sea and another on the other side of the bridge. A small museum has opened inside the palace. ✎ *Abu Dhabi-Dubai Rd; on the right before the bridge if driving from Dubai*

Saadiyat Island

Once a sleepy retreat for locals who liked to boat over to the island for a barbecue, Saadiyat Island (Island of Happiness) made international news when its re-development plans were unveiled. Set to be transformed into a world-class cultural, entertainment and leisure precinct, the island will be home to a new Guggen-heim Museum designed by Frank Gehry, a branch of the Louvre by Jean Nouvel, a performing arts centre by Zaha Hadid and a maritime museum by Tadao Ando. ✎ *www.saadiyat.ae*

Corniche & City Walk

Morning

🕙 Get a taxi in the early morning to the big flag pole at the tip of the **Breakwater** for views of the city skyline. Walk to the **Abu Dhabi Heritage Village** close by soon after opening, and spend time admiring the re-creations of old souqs, Bedouin camps and barasti living quarters. Stop by a coffee shop on the white sand beach overlooking the city for a refreshment. You'll need to pick up the pace for a brisk walk around the Breakwater and along the causeway to the **Emirates Palace**. Take time to admire the jaw-dropping interior and refuel at the elegant coffee shop. Then continue along the **Corniche**, stopping to catch stunning views of Lulu Island.

Afternoon

When you get to Sheikh Rashid bin Saeed Al Maktoum St (2nd St) you'll see the signs to **Central Market** – head down here to look at the giant white iconic statues of Abu Dhabi's beloved symbols – a coffee pot, cannon, incense burner and perfume sprinkler. From here, make your way back toward the breakwater and pop in for lunch at one of the InterContinental's many restaurants. Continue on to the *dhow*-building yards at Al Bateen, where crafts-men repair and build streamlined racing versions of the traditional wooden *dhow*. Head back to the hotel for a well-earned siesta and then return to the Corniche to watch the beautiful sunset.

Around Abu Dhabi

Left **The "AD Mall"** Centre **Khalifa Centre's exotic ware** Right **Marina Mall**

TOP 10 Places to Shop

Abu Dhabi Mall
Known popularly as "AD Mall", it has all the usual suspects when it comes to shops. ✆ *Map Q1 • Tourist Club area • 02 645 4858 • www.abudhabi-mall.com*

Marina Mall
This enormous mall is packed with stores, cinemas, cafés and an ice rink. ✆ *Map N5 • The Breakwater • 02 681 2310 • www.marinamall.ae*

Galleria
One of the city's newest additions, Galleria houses luxury boutique stores from across the world, spanning three floors. ✆ *Al Maryah Island • 02 616 6999*

Iranian Souq
Amidst the plastics and plants sold here, you'll find good Iranian painted crafts. ✆ *Map N1 • Mina (Port) Rd*

Carpet Souq
This is more about the experience, rather than the quality. Buy a *majlis* setting here. ✆ *Map N1 • Mina (Port) Rd*

Fotouh Al Khair Centre
Expats love this bright mini mall. It is home to Marks & Spencer (with a small but really good food hall), Monsoon and other popular UK brands. ✆ *Map P3 • Near Etisalat, opposite Cultural Foundation • 02 681 1130*

Khalifa Centre
Bargain for exquisite Persian rugs, sheeshas, tribal kilims or even silver prayer holders. ✆ *Map P1 • Tenth St, opp Abu Dhabi Mall, Tourist Club area • 02 667 9900*

Hamdan St
This local "high street" sells everything. It has jewellery stores and Arabic and Bollywood music shops as well as discount supermarkets. ✆ *Map P3 • Sheikh Hamdan bin Mohammed St (Hamdan St)*

Al Wahda Mall
With more than 250 stores and a cinema hall, this recently-expanded mall is now the largest in Abu Dhabi. ✆ *Near Central Bus Stop • 02 443 7000 • www.alwahda-mall.com*

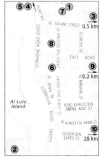

Dalma Mall
This mall is among the biggest in the city, with a mix of shops including Carrefour, Marks & Spencer, BHS, Home Center, Toys"R"Us, New Look and many others, plus a cinema and a Fun City. ✆ *Abu Dhabi–Tarif Hwy, opposite Mohammed Bin Zayed City • 02 550 6111 • www.dalmamall.ae*

Price Categories

For a three-course meal for one with half a bottle of wine (or equivalent meal), taxes and extra charges.

D	Under AED 25
DD	AED 25–100
DDD	AED 100–150
DDDD	AED 150–250
DDDDD	Over AED 250

Left **Interior of the upscale Sayad restaurant** Right **A belly dancer performing at Marakesh**

🔟 Restaurants

Bord Eau
This elegant French restaurant in the Shangri-La Qaryat Al Beri hotel (see p116) offers classic French dishes and also modern, innovative cuisine. There is an excellent wine list. ⬤ *Shangri-La Hotel, Qaryat Al Beri • 02 509 8511 • Open 6:30–11pm • DDDDD*

Etoiles
Best enjoyed during the months when you can sit on the pillared terrace, this is one of the most opulent restaurants in town, serving contemporary European dishes. ⬤ *Map N6 • Emirates Palace Hotel, Corniche West • 02 690 9000 • Open 7–11:30pm • DDDDD*

Sayad
Don't let the blue lighting and playful decor distract you too much from the fine seafood cuisine on offer at this swanky restaurant. ⬤ *Map N6 • Emirates Palace Hotel, Corniche West • 02 690 9000 • Open 6:30–11:30pm • DDDDD*

Vasco's
An incredible blend of European cooking, with a pinch of Asia, awaits you at this smart restaurant. ⬤ *Map P6 • Hilton Abu Dhabi, Corniche Rd West • 02 681 1900 • Open noon–3:30pm, 7–11pm • DDDD*

Shang Palace
Chinese cuisine cooked with panache and expertise. ⬤ *Shangri-La Hotel, Qaryat Al Beri • 02 509 8503 • Open noon–3pm & 7–11:30pm • DDDD*

La Mamma
The open kitchen turns out good, traditional Italian food. ⬤ *Map N1 • Sheraton Abu Dhabi Hotel & Resort • 02 697 0224 • Open noon–3:30pm & 7–11:30pm • DDDD*

Sardinia
Possibly Abu Dhabi's finest restaurant, the award-winning kitchen serves up top notch international cuisine that is beautifully presented. A complimentary amuse bouche is served between each course. ⬤ *Abu Dhabi Country Club • 02 657 7640 • Open noon–3pm, 7–11pm • DDDD*

Prego's
Sit on the terrace and enjoy delicious olive tapenade, hot breads and wood-fired pizzas. ⬤ *Map Q1 • Beach Rotana Tourist Club area • 02 697 9000 • Open noon–midnight • DDD*

Hakkassan
An award-winning Chinese eatery, Hakkasan offers exquisite Cantonese staples in opulent surroundings, designed by Gilles & Boissier. ⬤ *Map N6 • Emirates Palace Hotel, Corniche West St • 02 690 7999 • Open 6pm–midnight daily (also noon–3pm Fri–Sat) • DDDDD*

Marakesh
Savour authentic Moroccan cuisine at this opulent restaurant, while enjoying the belly dancer and Moroccan band. Try the succulent chicken lemon tajine. ⬤ *Map P2 • Millennium Hotel, Khalifa St • 02 614 6000 • Open 7pm–3am • DDDD*

➡️ *If bread and butter or olive oil are served at a restaurant, you can trust they'll be complimentary, but not so with water.*

Left **Soba's heavenly sashimi** Centre **Chefs at Lebanese Flower** Right **A lit-up India Palace**

Cheap Global Eats

Hanoi
The capital's original Vietnamese restaurant, serving classic unpretentious dishes. ☒ Map N2 • Khalifa Bin Zayed St • 02 626 1112 • Open 10am–11pm • DD

Beijing
Authentic Chinese food need not be expensive, as this popular spot proves. ☒ Map N2 • Madinat Zayed • 02 621 0708 • Open 11am–midnight • DD

Shamyat
You'll love the Syrian food, vine-covered ceiling and ladies baking traditional bread over a fire. ☒ Map N1 • Al Salam St, near Al Diar Regency Hotel • 02 671 2600 • Open 11am–midnight • DD; no alcohol

Pars Palace
Feast on exceptional Persian cuisine. Try the saffron rice with pomegranate seeds and kebabs with rich sauces. ☒ Map P4 • Al Araby St, Khalidiya, behind Corniche Towers • 02 681 8600 • Open 1–3:30pm & 6pm–midnight • DD; no alcohol

Soba
This sushi bar is ideal for a fast eat. The chefs are fun to watch and there's a DJ after 9pm. ☒ Map N2 • Le Royal Meridien Hotel, Khalifa St • 02 695 0450 • Open noon–3pm & 7pm–midnight • DDD

Royal Orchid
You'll be lured in by the fish tank under the floor and great Thai staples. ☒ Map P6 • Al Salam St • 02 677 9911 • Open noon–3pm & 7pm–midnight • DD; no alcohol

India Palace
Dine on North Indian cuisine in an opulent Raj decor. ☒ Map P1 • Al Salam St • 02 644 8777 • Open noon–midnight • DD; no alcohol

Lebanese Flower
A must-visit for scrumptious *mezze* (Arabic appetizers such as hommous and vine leaves), smoky mixed grilled meat plates, honey-soaked *baklava* and Turkish coffee. ☒ Map P3 • Near Choitrams Supermarket, cnr Hamdan & Fourth St, Khalidya • 02 665 8700 • Open 7am–3am • DD; no alcohol

Automatic
Grab a delicious chicken and garlic *shwarma* sandwich and a thick mango juice at this popular joint. ☒ Map P2 • Cnr Hamdan & Najda St • 02 676 9677 • Open 10am–1am • D; no alcohol

Arab Udupi
This popular branch of the chain of cheap Pakistani eateries dishes up saucy meat curries to a mixed crowd of expats. ☒ Map P2 • Behind BHS, off Hamdan St • 02 672 1522 • Open 24 hours • D; no alcohol

Price Categories

For a three-course meal for one with half a bottle of wine (or equivalent meal), taxes and extra charges.	**D** Under AED 25
	DD AED 25–100
	DDD AED 100–150
	DDDD AED 150–250
	DDDDD Over AED 250

Left **Al Fanar** Right **A cocktail maker in action at Trader Vic's**

🔟 Bars & Clubs

1 Cristal Cigar & Champagne Bar
For a sophisticated evening, stop by this "gentlemen's club" style bar for a glass of bubbly. 🄡 *Map P2* • *Millennium Hotel, Khalifa St* • *02 614 6000* • *Open 5pm–2am*

2 Jazz Bar & Dining
Enjoy live jazz as you dine or simply have a drink at this Art Deco-inspired bar. 🄡 *Map P6* • *Hilton Abu Dhabi, Corniche Rd West* • *02 681 1900* • *Open 7pm–1:30am*

3 Pearls & Caviar
Sip cocktails with Abu Dhabi's movers and shakers at this glitzy venue overlooking Maqta Creek. 🄡 *Shangri-La Hotel Qaryat Al Beri* • *02 509 8777* • *Open 7:30pm–midnight*

4 Al Fanar
Enjoy the views while sipping a cocktail at this revolving rooftop restaurant and bar. 🄡 *Map N2* • *Le Royal Meridien* • *02 695 0490* • *Open 12:30–3pm all days; 7–11pm Fri–Wed & 7pm–midnight Thu*

5 Trader Vic's
Kickstart the night with a lethal cocktail – in a big glass with umbrellas – at this Polynesian-themed bar and restaurant. 🄡 *Map Q1* • *Beach Rotana Hotel, Tourist Club Area* • *02 697 9011* • *Open 12:30–3:30pm & 7–11:30pm*

6 Oceans
Chill out on big white cushions on high-backed cane sofas at this breezy lounge bar. If it is too hot outside, head in to the cool colonial-style interior. 🄡 *Map N2* • *Le Royal Meridien, Khalifa St* • *02 674 1094* • *Open noon–1:30am*

7 Allure by Cipriani
The dance and drinks terrace overlooking the Abu Dhabi Grand Prix circuit is the place to be seen. 🄡 *Yas Marina Yacht Club, Abu Dhabi* • *02 657 5400* • *Open Wed–Fri 11pm–late*

8 Eight
Classy joint with long sofas and excellent cocktails. 🄡 *Souk Qaryat Al Beri, Bain Al Jessrain* • *02 558 1988* • *Open 10pm–3am*

9 Left Bank
This intimate bar with a kitsch interior offers stunning views of the Sheikh Zayed Mosque from outside. 🄡 *Souq Qaryat Al Beri* • *02 558 1680* • *Open 6pm–midnight Sun–Thu, noon–midnight Fri–Sat*

10 Chameleon
This chic cocktail bar is one of the classiest venues in the city, with prices to match. Enjoy beautiful views of the creek with your drink. 🄡 *Fairmont Bab Al Bahr, Between the Bridges* • *02 654 3238* • *Open 6pm–1am Tue–Sun*

Left **P J O'Reilly's Irish pub** Centre **The 49ers horseshoe emblem** Right **Brauhaus' German brews**

TOP 10 Expat Pubs

Hemingways
The stale beer smell and smoke is part of this popular institution's attraction. ◎ *Map P6 • Hilton Abu Dhabi Hotel, Corniche West • 02 681 1900 • Open noon–midnight*

Brauhaus
Have a German beer with old-timers on a lazy afternoon. ◎ *Map Q1 • Beach Rotana Hotel, Tourist Club area • 02 697 9011 • Open 4pm–1am*

Heroes
Great table service ensures you'll always get a drink at this sports bar, no matter how packed it is. ◎ *Map P2 • Crowne Plaza Hotel, Sheikh Hamdan bin Mohammed St • 02 621 7444 • Open noon–4am*

P J O'Reilly's
This Irish pub keeps everyone happy with its "pub grub" and friendly staff. ◎ *Map N2 • Le Royal Meridien, Khalifa St • 02 674 2020 • Open noon–3am*

Captain's Arms
Get cosy inside this traditional English pub or lounge on its sunny garden outside. ◎ *Map P1 • Le Meridien Abu Dhabi, Tourist Club area • 02 644 6666 • Open noon–midnight*

The Harvester's Pub
You'll see a rowdy crowd leaving their dartboards to enjoy an on-screen match at this smoky basement bar. ◎ *Map P2 • Al Diar Sands Hotel, Zayed the First St • 02 633 5335 / 615 6666 • Open noon–midnight*

The Tavern
A replica of a smart English pub, The Tavern has good service and a popular Friday brunch. ◎ *Map N1 • Sheraton Abu Dhabi Hotel & Resort, Al Markaziyah • 02 677 3333 • Open noon–1am Sat–Tue, noon–2am Wed–Fri*

49ers
Head here early as this pub, subtitled "the Gold Rush", gets packed, particularly when there's a band on. ◎ *Map P2 • Al Diar Dana Hotel, Zayed the First St • 02 645 8000 • Open noon–3:30am*

Rock Bottom Café
The big juicy steaks, good live music, a boisterous atmosphere and discounted beverages will keep you coming back for more. ◎ *Map P1 • Al Diar Capital Hotel, Hamdan Bin Mohammed St • 02 678 7700 • Open noon–3am*

Ally Pally Corner
Head to this typical English pub for Guinness and to hear Gulf War stories and tales of pre-oil times from the city's older expat males. ◎ *Map N2 • Al Ain Palace Hotel, The Corniche East • 02 679 4777 • Open noon–1:30am*

Left **Marina Mall** Centre **Hitting the Corniche for a walk** Right **Emirates Palace's opulent interiors**

TOP 10 Best of the Rest

Corniche walk
Pack your walking shoes and schedule your saunter down Abu Dhabi's splendid Corniche for the late afternoon so you won't miss the spectacular sunsets *(see pp88–91)*.

Hamdan Street
Bustling neon-lit Hamdan Street doesn't have the stylish shops of the swish shopping malls but its vibrant atmosphere, best appreciated at night, make it a more interesting place to shop *(see p92)*.

Go shopping
Laidback Abu Dhabi is a more relaxing place to shop than Dubai, and the air-conditioned malls provide relief from the heat. Evenings are best, when local Emiratis love to shop.

Emirates Palace tour
Not staying at this opulent hotel? Then a tour is a must. You can explore yourself but a guided tour ensures you don't miss a single detail and includes afternoon tea *(see pp22–3)*.

Palace drive
Take a taxi or hire a car to explore impressive Al Bateen neighbourhood. The colossal Sheikhs' palaces, their high walls, verdant gardens and armoured vehicles make for a memorable experience. ✪ *Map Q5 • Al Bateen area • Taxi AED20, hire car from AED150 per day*

City skyline view
Spectacular views of the city's Manhattan-like skyline can be enjoyed from the big flag pole at the end of the Breakwater *(see pp88–91)*.

Cruise
The stunning Corniche and Abu Dhabi skyline are best appreciated from the sea. Savour the fresh seafood and sparkling city views from Le Royal Meridien's sleek Shuja Yacht on a cruise. ✪ *Map N5 • Departs from the Marina at The Broadwater • 02 674 2020 • Times vary: sunset and dinner cruises (8–11pm) • Adm*

Sunset drinks at Al Fanar
Enjoy a bird's eye view of this stunning city of skyscrapers as you sip a cocktail and watch the sun set from this stylish revolving restaurant *(see p95)*.

Ghantoot Racing & Polo Club
Watch Emirati and Argentine polo teams practice or play an exciting match on sprawling landscaped lawns. ✪ *Ghantoot Racing & Polo Club, Dubai-Abu Dhabi Rd • 02 562 9050 • Nov–Apr*

Dine at Jazz Bar
Enjoy an exquisite meal while listening to fabulous live jazz – often performed by excellent South African bands – at this Abu Dhabi institution. Book in advance for weekends *(see p95)*.

 Following pages **The Heritage Village Museum, Abu Dhabi**

STREETSMART

DUBAI & ABU DHABI'S TOP 10

Left **A sunny day at the beach** Right **Deira City Centre mall**

TOP 10 Planning Your Trip

Passports & Visa
Complimentary 30-day visit visas are available on arrival at UAE airport immigration desks. Passports must be valid for 6 months from the date of entry to the UAE. Visas can be extended at the Department of Naturalisation and Residency (Tel: 04 398 0000, 02 398 1010).
⊘ *Visa free; visa extension AED 620 for 30 days*
• www.dnrd.gov.ae

Insurance
While petty crime is extremely rare in the UAE, insurance covering loss of luggage and theft is always good to have, along with comprehensive health and dental insurance. Hospitals are very efficient, but the services are expensive.

When to Go
Winter is usually when Dubai is at its best. This is when the Dubai Shopping Festival, Global Village and most major international sporting events take place. In recent years though, the UAE has had cool, grey, wet winters. So those wanting guaranteed sunshine should visit during Oct–Nov or Mar–Apr instead. Summer is best avoided.

What to Take
Bring swimwear, a hat and sun block (expensive in the UAE) for the beach. Loose linen and cotton clothes are best for sightseeing. Make sure they're not transparent – remember, it's a conservative country, so you need to dress modestly. Pack a cardigan or sweater as most indoor places are air-conditioned.

How Long to Stay
While Dubai makes a great 2–3 day stopover on your way somewhere, 5 days to a week is wonderful if you want to relax at a beach resort, do some serious shopping in the souqs and malls, as well as take in the sights of Dubai Creek, Al Fahidi and Shindagha. Add 1–2 days to visit Abu Dhabi.

Electricity
UAE power sockets generally accept the UK three prong plug operating on 220/240 volts, although you may also see the European two round prong plug. It's not a bad idea to bring an adaptor that works for both. Most good hotels will have adaptors you can borrow, or you can buy them in local supermarkets.

Customs & Duty Free
The duty free allowance is 400 cigarettes or 2 kg of tobacco, cigars to the value of AED 3000 and 4 litres of wine or spirits. It's illegal to purchase alcohol in the UAE without a liquor license (only available to UAE residents), so buy duty free at the airport if you want to have sunset drinks on the balcony but want to avoid expensive mini-bar costs.

Prohibited Items
In addition to the items on most countries blacklists, such as firearms, illegal drugs and pornography, it is forbidden to bring in any banned movies, TV programs and offensive publications, especially films and programs that may include scenes with passionate kissing, sex, nudity or semi-nudity, drug use or any content relating to Israel.

Time Zone
The UAE time zone is GMT+4. It is 6 hours behind Australian Eastern Standard Time. There is no daylight saving.

Opening Hours & Weekends
The UAE weekend is Friday and Saturday. Business hours aren't fixed, but generally, shopping malls open 10am–10pm Sat–Thu, opening in the late afternoon and evening on Fridays. Shops in the streets open approximately the same times but close for lunch from 1–4/5pm. Government departments open around 7am and close to the public around 3pm.

  Dubai has several good local English-language TV stations. Most hotel rooms feature global satellite channels like CNN and BBC.

Left **An Emirates Airlines flight** Centre **Local papers & magazines** Right **Dubai Visitor Info logo**

ᵀᴼᴾ10 Travel Information Sources

UAE Interact
The excellent website of the UAE Ministry for Information and Culture is easy to use. It covers everything you need to know about the UAE from daily news and useful information to fascinating articles on aspects of Emirati culture, with downloadable annual reports and short videos. ⬥ www.uaeinteract.com

UAE Federal Government Portal
The UAE government's official portal is a handy resource for official matters like visas and red tape, but there's also plenty of information on travel safety, flight times, medical services and consumer rights, which is aimed more at tourists than expats or residents. ⬥ www.government.ae

Dubai Tourism & Commerce Marketing
Look here for a wide range of information for travellers, from destination content and accommodation listings, to more interesting coverage on local culture, sights, shopping and other things to do. ⬥ www.dubaitourism.ae

Sheikh Mohammed's Website
The fascinating website of the visionary UAE Prime Minister and Ruler of Dubai, Sheikh Mohammed bin Rashid Al Maktoum, has comprehensive information on the UAE, as well as sections featuring the Sheikh's poetry and wisdom. The website lets you write an email to the Sheikh and receive a royal response! ⬥ www.sheikhmohammed.com

UAE Airlines
Access destination information, check timetables, book flights online or even hire a car on the websites of UAE's airlines – Etihad Airline (www.etihad.com), Emirates Airline (www.emirates.com) and budget airlines Air Arabia (www.airarabia.com) and flydubai (www.flydubai.com).

Emirates News Agency (WAM)
Spend some time trawling through the news releases on this site. You'll dig up everything from which world leader the UAE President sent a telegram to that day, to the changes to property laws. ⬥ www.wam.org.ae

Media
The UAE has a number of dreadful newspapers which print government press releases word for word. Much more interesting are the free newspaper 7 Days, and the excellent The National. ⬥ Dh2 for most newspapers

Entertainment Media
Time Out Dubai and Time Out Abu Dhabi magazines include comprehensive listings for arts and cultural events, restaurants, bars, clubs and sporting activities. The Time Out website is also a great source of information so you can plan and buy tickets to big events online. Expat-focused What's On magazine is also good. ⬥ AED 5 for Time Out magazine • www.timeoutdubai.com; www.timeoutabudhabi.com; www.timeouttickets.com

Dubai Tourism Info Centre
If sightseeing along Deira Creek or shopping in the souqs, head to the main tourism office on Baniyas Square, in a traditional-looking windtower building, for information. The Info Centre also provides many online services and directories. ⬥ Map L2 • Baniyas Square, Deira • www.dubaitourism.ae

Abu Dhabi Tourism Authority
This website is a great starting point for anyone looking to visit the capital. It covers everything from events and landmarks to malls, souqs and beaches. There are "must see" lists for those on a tight schedule, and plenty of images and videos. ⬥ www.visitabudhabi.ae

 You'll find the excellent complimentary Concierge and Visitor magazines in most five-star hotel rooms.

Left **The Abu Dhabi Airport terminal** Right **Abu Dhabi's Al Ghazal taxi**

🔟 Arriving in Dubai & Abu Dhabi

1 Dubai International Airport
Sleek Dubai Airport is one of the world's best. Emirates Airline has its own, ultramodern terminal (3), which, along with Terminal 1, is connected to the Dubai Metro. If you're from one of the 32 countries eligible for an on-the-spot visa, the process is a breeze. ☏ 04 224 5555
• www.dubaiairport.com

2 Abu Dhabi International Airport
All planes pull into Abu Dhabi airport's attractive mushroom-shaped satellite, so you don't have far to walk to Immigration and the baggage carousel beyond. Service is efficient, and if you come from one of the 32 countries eligible for visas on arrival, the process is quick. ☏ 02 575 7500
• www.abudhabiairport.ae

3 Marhaba & Golden Class Services
To enjoy five-star service or for special assistance, organize to be met by the Marhaba Service in Dubai or Golden Class in Abu Dhabi. For a fee, a hostess greets you on arrival, whisks you through a special immigration line, helps you with your luggage, and escorts you to your transport. ☏ Golden Class, Abu Dhabi: 02 575 7466
• Marhaba Service, Dubai: 04 224 5780

4 Immigration
One way to help immigration procedures go smoothly is to greet officials in Arabic. Try "As'salam Alaykum" ("Peace be upon you") to which they should warmly respond: "Wa'alaykum salaam" (literally meaning "and peace right back to you"). If you don't come from a country eligible for an on-the-spot visa, make sure you have your UAE embassy-issued visa documents.

5 Duty-Free & Customs
There are duty-free shops at Arrivals at Dubai and Abu Dhabi airports. After collecting your luggage choose the "Nothing to Declare" or "Declare" exit. Customs officers randomly select passengers to put their luggage through the X-ray machine again or may ask you to open your bags. The UEA has very strict narcotics laws, and some prescription drugs are banned from coming into the country. Check with your embassy before flying, as you may have to ask your doctor for documentation (see p106). ☏ www.customs.ae

6 Arrivals Hall
Once through Customs, you'll come to the Arrivals Hall, which is jam-packed with desks representing tourism agencies, car rental companies, hotel desks, an accommodation booking service, ATMs and mobile phone retailers. It would be a good idea to get some cash from the ATM here for the taxi to your hotel.

7 Dubai Airport Taxis
It isn't difficult to find a taxi at Dubai's airport. The flag fall is AED 25 from the airport. The fare into Deira is around AED 35, to Bur Dubai AED 35–45 and to Jumeirah AED 55–75. ☏ Dubai Transport • 04 208 0808
• www.dtc.dubai.ae

8 Abu Dhabi Airport Taxis
The TransAD (Abu Dhabi) taxis outside Abu Dhabi's airport ferry you to the city centre for around AED 65–75.
☏ 600 535353

9 Dubai Airport Bus
Budget travellers can use the convenient Airport Bus Service. The 401 goes to Union Square, Baniyas Rd, Al-Sabkha bus station and Deira bus station. The 402 travels via Deira City Centre to Karama, Mankhool and Bur Dubai. Both cost around AED 3.

🔟 Abu Dhabi Airport Bus
The 901 travels between Abu Dhabi airport and the town centre 24-hours a day. During the day it leaves every 30 minutes and in the evening every 45 minutes. Tickets can be purchased on the bus for AED 3.

 Taxis can be reluctant to hand over change. Leave a few coins if the driver has helped you with your luggage and been courteous.

Left **An abra ride** Right **A local bus**

TOP10 Getting Around

Car Rental
There are car rental desks in the Arrivals halls of the airports and also at most hotels. Europcar offers the best prices as well as a drop-off and pick-up service.
⊗ *Europcar: Abu Dhabi 02 626 1441; Dubai 04 220 3033 • Thrifty: Abu Dhabi 02 575 7400; Dubai 04 800 4694 • Budget: Abu Dhabi 02 443 8430; Dubai 04 295 6667*

Driving Conditions & Road Rules
Only the brave drive in the UAE, which has one of the highest road death rates in the world. Drive on the right side of the road. Unless otherwise signposted, speed limits are 60km/h on city streets, 80km/h on major city roads, and 100–120km/h on highways. Do not drink and drive. There is a zero-tolerance policy – if caught, you're sure to spend the night in jail.

Dubai Taxis
There are taxi ranks at shopping malls. Elsewhere, flag them down on the street. All taxis use meters. The flag fall is AED 3 by day, and AED 6 at night. A short taxi ride in Deira or Bur Dubai might cost you AED 10, from Deira to Sheikh Zayed Rd around AED 15, or from Bur Dubai to Jumeirah Beach from AED 25–45. ⊗ *Dubai Transport: 04 208 0808 • www.dtc.dubai.ae*

Abu Dhabi Taxis
Regular taxis are cheap in Abu Dhabi. A short ride in the city will cost from AED 3–15. Flag taxis down on the street. During peak times from 8–9am and 5–6pm, weekend evenings and prayer times, when it's impossible to find a taxi, phone ahead and book one through the upmarket but expensive Al Ghazal service.

Dubai Bus Service
The bus service has 79 routes around Dubai. Details of routes are available on the Roads and Transport Authority's (RTA) website www.rta.ae. It includes a helpful "journey planner". Fares range from AED 1–3.
⊗ *04 800 90 90 (Open 24 hours)*

Inter-Emirate Bus Service
The RTA also runs a bus service to other emirates. Frequent services operate from 6am to midnight daily from bus stations in Deira (for northern emirates) and Bur Dubai (to Abu Dhabi and Al Ain).

Long Distance Taxis
There are long-distance shared taxi services from Dubai and Abu Dhabi bus stations to all emirates. Taxis leave when they're full. Fares are similar to the buses but taxis are faster. Not all have air-conditioning, and they can get cramped. Dubai Transport operates a shared taxi to Abu Dhabi for AED 50. ⊗ *Dubai Transport: 04 208 0808*

Metro
Dubai's impressive, driverless metro began service in 2009 and has become an integral part of the city, linking up areas difficult to get to by car. Single journeys are inexpensive – only AED 2. ⊗ *www.rta.ae*

Abras
The abras continually criss-cross Dubai Creek connecting Deira and Bur Dubai from 5am to midnight daily. The fare is AED 1 per person. You can hire your own abra to cruise the Creek for AED 100 an hour. Docks are handily situated at Bur Dubai Souq, Deira Spice Souq, Al Sabkha, Al Seef Park and Dubai Municipality. ⊗ *04 800 9090*

Walking
There are few places that are walkable in Dubai and Abu Dhabi, apart from Dubai's souqs, marinas and Al Fahidi and Abu Dhabi's Corniche. Elsewhere, be cautious on pedestrian crossings, which drivers ignore. Walking is better in the cooler winter months. In the scorching heat of summer, it's not advisable as there is little shelter from the sun.

➤ *A ride on an abra across bustling Dubai Creek is for many a highlight of a trip to Dubai – make sure you do it at least once!*

Left **An exchange centre sign** Centre **An Emirates Post mail box** Right **A prepaid phone card**

TOP 10 Banking & Communications

1 Currency

The UAE's currency is the UAE dirham, written as AED (Arab Emirates Dirham) or as Dh. One dirham is divided into 100 fils. Notes are in denominations of AED 5, AED 10, AED 20, AED 50, AED 100, AED 200, AED 500 and AED 1000. Coins are available as 25 fils, 50 fils as well as one dirham.

2 Exchange Rates

The UAE dirham is pegged to the US dollar. US$1 is equal to AED 3.67. All other currencies fluctuate, but at the time of writing €1 was equal to AED 5 and £1 was worth AED 5.75.

3 Banks & ATMs

Numerous international banks operate in the UAE, including HSBC, Citibank and Standard Chartered Bank. Good local banks include National Bank of Abu Dhabi, Mashreq Bank and National Bank of Dubai. Globally linked ATMs are everywhere, allowing you access to your home account.

4 Credit Cards & Travellers' Cheques

While travellers' cheques can be changed in the UAE, credit cards are preferred. Visa, American Express and Mastercard are widely accepted and credit cards can be used almost everywhere. If using travellers' cheques, opt for Thomas Cook, which has local branches.

5 Calling the UAE

To phone the UAE from abroad, dial your international access code, the UAE country code 971, then 4 for Dubai or 2 for Abu Dhabi, followed by the local number. To dial a mobile from abroad, dial 971 50/55 followed by the mobile number. Within the UAE, dial 050/055 for mobiles, 04 to call Dubai from outside the emirate and 02 to phone Abu Dhabi from another emirate.

6 Mobile Phones

Etisalat is the national telecommunications company. Etisalat's excellent "Ahlan: Visitors Mobile Package" for cell phones costs AED 60, lasts 90 days and is available at the Etisalat kiosks, grocery stores, petrol stations and street kiosks. *www.etisalat.ae*

7 Phone Cards

Buy an AED 20 Pre-Paid Card to make calls from public phones in the UAE, to make calls to the UAE from other countries and to pay for Wi-Fi internet services at Etisalat iZone Hot Spots. *www.etisalat.ae*

8 Internet Access

Etisalat's wireless Internet (Wi-Fi) service can be accessed at iZone Hotspots at airports, shopping malls, coffee shops, restaurants and business centres. A prepaid card costs AED 15 an hour, AED 30 for 3 hours, AED 70 for 24 hours or AED 120 for a 60-day stay. Internet cafés are widely available in the cities.

9 Post Offices

Emirates Post is the UAE's national postal service. You can buy stamps at any post office and at some stationery shops. Mail to Europe, North America and Australasia takes about 10 days. It's unreliable, however, so register anything valuable or use a courier for anything urgent. *Dubai Main Post Office: 04 262 2222 • Abu Dhabi Central Post Office: 02 621 1611 • Main post offices: Open 8am–10pm Sat–Thu, 8am–noon Fri • www.emiratespost.com*

10 Shipping & Couriers

Emirates Post provides surface and air delivery services for sending large parcels. See their website for details. Courier services are more reliable. Companies with a good reputation for service include Aramex, FedEx and DHL. All will pick-up from your hotel – you can pay on pick-up if you don't have an account. *Aramex: 600 544 000 • FedEx: 800 33339 • DHL: 800 4004 • www.emiratespost.com*

Left **An Emirati woman** Centre **A local mosque** Right **A session of "Open Doors, Open Minds"**

℡10 Things to be Aware of

Languages
Arabic is the official language, although English is widely spoken. As 80% of the population are foreign, you'll hear scores of languages on the street. Signage is generally in both Arabic and English.

Islam
The UAE is an Islamic state following a tolerant version of Sharia Law, with both Sharia and civil law courts. UAE Muslims adhere to the conduct of Islam, praying five times a day, donating to charity, fasting and doing the pilgrimage to Mecca.

Call-to-prayer
If you stay in Deira, Bur Dubai or the Al Fahidi area in particular, you'll hear the beautiful sound of the call-to-prayer echoing through the streets five times a day. Broadcast from the minarets of mosques, the call-to-prayer beckons Muslims to come and worship.

Respectful Conduct
Never shake hands with an Emirati woman unless offered her hand first. If visiting someone's home, remove your shoes, don't show the soles of your feet and don't eat with your left hand. Displays of affection among couples in public are frowned upon. While holding hands is acceptable, passionate kissing and embracing is not. Rude gestures and swearing are offensive.

Photographing Women
Photographing Emirati and other Muslim women is not acceptable without asking their permission first. Even at places where covered ladies prepare local food for sale as part of the displays, ask first before taking their photo. Photography of Sheikhs' palaces, police and military buildings, ports and airports is forbidden.

Dress Code
Visitors should dress modestly. Loose long linen or cotton clothing is respectful and is also suited to the scorching heat. Women should not wear tight or transparent clothing, skirts above the knee, sleeveless tops, halter-necks or shoestring straps in public, while men should refrain from wearing shorts and sleeveless tops. In Sharjah, wearing these clothes in public can incur a severe penalty.

Pork
Muslims do not eat pork, however, pork products are for sale to non-Muslims in "Pork Rooms" in supermarkets such as Spinneys. Most restaurants at five-star hotels include pork on their menus.

Alcohol
It's illegal to purchase alcohol without a liquor license (only available to UAE residents) so buy alcohol at the airport duty free shop. You can drink alcohol in hotels and licensed venues. Penalties for drunken behaviour in public are heavy. Sharjah is a dry emirate – alcohol is not sold or allowed there.

Sheikh Mohammed Centre for Cultural Understanding
This organization runs a number of activities under the "Open Doors, Open Minds" program, which is aimed at promoting tolerance of culture and religion. Stop at the Al Fahidi courtyard house to book a tour (see pp 12–13).

Ramadan & Islamic holidays
Religious festivals rely on the sighting of the moon. Alcohol is not served the night before a religious holiday. During the holy month of Ramadan, government offices operate on shorter hours, most shops close during the day, and eating, drinking and smoking in public is forbidden. There is no music or dancing either. After *Iftar* (breaking of the fast), the mood is festive – malls stay open until midnight and the celebratory spirit is infectious.

Left **Soft drink vending machines** Centre **"Camel Crossing" road sign** Right **A beach warning**

TOP 10 Things to Avoid

Dehydration
Whether lying by the pool or walking around town, you're equally at risk of dehydrating in the UAE's ferocious heat. To avoid dehydration, wear light clothes, avoid the sun in the hottest part of the day and drink much more water than you normally would at home.

Traffic Accidents
Dubai's traffic is horrific. Be vigilant as a pedestrian and as a passenger don't be embarrassed to ask your driver to "*shway shway!*" (slow down!).

Rush Hour
Don't think about going anywhere in Dubai from 8–10am (when commuters head to work), noon–2pm (when they go home or out for lunch) and from 4–6:30pm. Also avoid the roads around 8–9pm on Thursday and Friday nights, when everyone seems to be going out.

Parking & Speeding Tickets
UAE parking and traffic cops take their jobs very seriously. Look out for speed signs, particularly in areas where there are road works. Always look for parking signs and orange parking metres wherever you park, especially at night. Otherwise, expect to return to a parking ticket on your windscreen.

Road Surprises!
While you might find those "Road Surprises!" signs amusing the first time you see them (and everyone loves to stop to take a photo of the camel sign), they're there for a reason. Slow down and look out for dips, speed bumps and sand on the road. And while they're very cute, camels can be troublesome – they just love to take a stroll on the freeway.

Driving in Rain & Sand Storms
Rainy weather makes driving hazardous simply because UAE residents aren't used to driving in the rain, so they won't necessarily slow down. The rate of accidents is considerably higher in wet weather. Decelerate or pull over in sand storms when visibility is poor. When you see oncoming drivers with their hazard lights on, it means conditions are even worse up ahead.

Swimming Dangers
When you see signs warning bathers about dangerous rips and strong undertows, these should be taken seriously. Avoid swimming if you're not a strong swimmer, or take extra care. Despite the calm appearance of the water, Dubai's beaches have very powerful undercurrents.

Souq Spruikers
The most annoying thing about shopping in the souqs is the spruiking. Touts aggressively attempt to lure customers into shops to buy "copy watches, copy bags, Madam!" Unless you want to buy these counterfeit goods (great value but illegal), the best strategy is to ignore them completely. Show even the slightest bit of interest or politeness, and they'll never leave you alone.

Drugs
Do not attempt to bring drugs into the country. Keep in mind that even some prescription drugs, such as codeine, and anti-depressant and HRT medications are banned *(see p102)*. The UAE has a zero tolerance policy on drugs. Penalties and sentences are harsh. While the death penalty is an option, it's rarely applied. However, you're more likely to serve a long sentence and get deported.

Prostitutes
If you stay in Bur Dubai neighbourhoods such as Mankhool, you might see prostitutes on the streets at night, often from China and former Soviet countries. They also frequent many bars and nightclubs in Deira and Bur Dubai. Prostitution is illegal and prostitutes are best avoided.

Left **Year-round sunshine at Dubai beaches** Right **Signs for public conveniences**

🔟 Useful Information

Business & Shopping Hours
The official weekend is Friday and Saturday. Everyone has a day off on the main Friday prayer day, while some work half or full days on Saturday. Government departments open 7:30am–3pm while private companies work 9am–6pm. Supermarkets open 8am–10pm while major malls open 10am–10pm. Smaller malls and independent shops do not open until the afternoon on Fridays.

Climate
The UAE has an arid sub-tropical climate with infrequent rainfall. The country was synonymous with year-round sunshine until the 2006 winter, one of the wettest on record. Temperatures average 20 degrees Celsius in winter to 45 degrees Celsius in summer.

Weights & Measures
The UAE uses the metric system, except for petrol, when it uses gallons. A wide range of measurement systems are used for clothes and shoes which are manufactured in Europe, Asia, the Middle East and North America.

Taxes
Residents of the UAE don't pay income tax. This is a big incentive for expats to build a life here. The only taxes here are on alcohol and the municipality and service taxes on hotel rooms.

Photography & Video
Emiratis are obsessed with technology so if you're after something new you'll find a wide range of well-priced digital cameras. If you need additional memory cards, tapes or batteries try the myriad electronics stores in City Centre and Baniyas Square, Deira.

Smoking
UAE legislation introduced in 2004 provided for a ban on smoking in public places, including shopping malls, restaurants and entertainment venues. Unfortunately this has not been enforced. By law, restaurants are required to have non-smoking sections but most don't. At the time of research the UAE was set to enforce laws and give officials power to issue on-the-spot fines to lawbreakers.

Homosexuality
Homosexuality is illegal and homosexual practices are punishable with harsh penalties. You'll see men from Central Asia and the Indian Subcontinent holding hands – this does not mean they are gay; they are just good friends. Likewise, you'll see Emirati men rub noses when they meet, in the same way that close male friends kiss cheeks in Europe's Mediterranean countries.

Women Travellers
Women travelling solo in the UAE shouldn't experience any harassment if they follow local norms. They should sit in the back seat of taxis, in the "women's section" of buses and eat in "family rooms" in cheap hotels. Dedicated women's queues at banks and government departments mean women get preferential service.

Contraceptives
Contraceptives can be purchased in pharmacies in the UAE without a prescription. They'll generally be kept on the shelves alongside women's hygiene products. The price is comparable to Europe and Australasia.

Toilets
All shopping centres, five-star hotels and good restaurants and bars have clean toilets – it's okay to walk off the street to use these. In shopping centres and cheaper street eateries you may come across "hole in the ground" Oriental toilets alongside Western toilets. You will also find bidets or a hose for ablutions.

 All restaurants charge municipality tax and service tax, which totals to 17.5 per cent.

Left **Pedestrian crossing sign** Centre **A local bottled water brand** Right **A traffic policeman**

TOP 10 Security & Health

Precautions
The biggest danger to your health and wellbeing in the UAE is the heat. Take precautions to avoid dehydration, sunburn and sunstroke. From June to August in particular, avoid walking as much as possible and take advantage of the cheap air-conditioned taxis.

Personal Safety
While petty crime is unheard of, be sensible – don't dress like a tourist and don't flash cash around. The most dangerous place is on the road. The UAE has one of the highest rates of road deaths on the planet. As a pedestrian be vigilant; drivers will not stop for you on a crossing, so cross only at lights where possible. If your taxi driver is driving too fast or recklessly, tell him to slow down.

Drinking Water & Food Safety
The tap water is safe to drink. At most, you may experience an upset tummy for a couple of days as your body adjusts to new bacteria. When eating street food, only try eateries popular with locals.

Consulates
Generally, embassies are in Abu Dhabi and consulates in Dubai, although there are a few exceptions. Check your consulate's UAE website for travel warnings and security information. Consulate phone numbers are listed in the Etisalat phone directory that is available in most hotel rooms.

Emergency Info
In case of emergency, phone the following numbers: Police 999; Ambulance 998/999; Fire Department 997; Operator 181.

If You Get Arrested
The UAE is an Islamic state and you can land in trouble for not respecting religious customs and decency laws. Under absolutely no condition drink alcohol and drive. In Sharjah, it's illegal for women to travel in a vehicle with men other than their husband. Women must dress modestly and not show their décolletage, upper arms or back. In Dubai and Abu Dhabi, arrests have resulted from foreigners being too affectionate in public, particularly during Ramadan. If you get arrested, do not sign anything in Arabic immediately. Your consulate should be your first call – they can help facilitate contact with a local bilingual lawyer.

Road Traffic Accidents
If you're in an accident, first get out of harm's way, then call the police (999) for instructions. Do not move the car unless instructed to do so by the police. If another party is involved and you have your camera handy, take photos for insurance purposes.

Hospitals
Hospital standards are outstanding in the UAE at both private and public hospitals. You will find that the service is faster at emergency departments at private hospitals. ✎ Dubai: American Hospital 04 336 7777, Al Zahra Private Medical Centre 04 331 5000 • Abu Dhabi: Gulf Diagnostic Centre 02 665 8090, Centre Medical Franco-Emirien 02 626 5722

Dental
The UAE has excellent dentists and consultations are reasonably priced. ✎ Dubai: British Dental Clinic 04 342 1318, American Dental Clinic 04 344 0668 • Abu Dhabi: British Dental Clinic 02 677 3308, Advanced Dental Clinic 02 681 2921

Pharmacies
There are many pharmacies in Dubai and Abu Dhabi that are open 24 hours. The daily newspapers list them. However, in Dubai, you can phone 04 223 2323 to find out the pharmacy nearest to you that's open, and in Abu Dhabi call 02 777 929.

 Global media surveys frequently place the UAE in the top 20 safest destinations.

Left **Enjoy a walk through the Bastakiya** Right **An abra ride is a cheap way to cross the Creek**

🔟 Budget Tips

When Not to Go

Avoid Dubai and Abu Dhabi during major events and conferences unless it's something you actually want to go to!) when hotel room prices go through the roof. While December and January are the coolest months, winter is the peak season and hotels charge rack rates. Ramadan is another period to avoid.

Summer Savings

While summer is best avoided due to the ferocious heat, this is the ideal time for budget travellers. Most hotels drop their rates by 50% and offer excellent holiday packages. The Summer Surprises shopping festival means there are great bargains to be found.

Internet Deals

Travellers averse to package deals can find great deals on the internet if they can be flexible. Accommodation websites such as Expedia offer great hotels at bargain prices, particularly in the quiet periods between big events and conferences. Hotel websites, such as the Accor site, are also a great source for discounted rooms.

Transport

Budget travellers can save money by catching the *abra* across Dubai Creek. These open-sided wooden boats cost just AED 1 per trip and connect Dubai's main sights in Deira and Bur Dubai. The buses are a cheap alternative to taxis *(see p103)*.

Supermarkets

The supermarkets are excellent in the UAE. It's possible to find products from all over the world. Carrefour has a reputation for having the lowest prices. It also has the best bakery with delicious Middle Eastern pastries and an excellent deli counter where you buy olives, cheeses and cold meats for picnics and balcony snacks while you enjoy the sunset.

Brunches & Buffets

The Friday Brunch is a ritual for many expats. Five star hotels offer great value all-you-can-eat-and-drink brunches, including alcohol, from AED 70–200 per person. Similar mid-week buffet lunches and dinners are also great value, starting from as low as AED 47. Check local magazines for the latest offers.

Cheap Eats

A couple of *shwarmas* and a fresh mango juice make a great cheap eat. *Shwarmas* cost around AED 3 and juices from AED 6. If you're after something more filling, head to one of Dubai and Abu Dhabi's many cheap ethnic eateries *(see p64)* where you can spend as little as AED 30 per person for a curry or biryani or a few mezze dishes and a mixed Arabic grill.

Happy Hours

While alcohol is expensive in the UAE (it's the only thing that is taxed), you can drink cheaply if you take advantage of happy hours (generally from 6pm–8pm) and drink promotions. Many bars and clubs offer half-price drinks, two-for-one deals, two free drinks or "free bubbly for the ladies", on particular nights.

Free Stuff to Do

In Dubai, a walk through the Al Fahidi neighbourhood or on Shindagha waterfront is free, while it costs nothing to stroll along Abu Dhabi's beautiful Corniche.

Discounts & Bargaining

Bargaining is expected in the souqs and carpet shops. Make an offer at half the price and work up from there. In electronics and jewellery stores, it's acceptable to ask if that's the best price or for a discount if you pay cash or buy two. Let them know if you found something cheaper elsewhere and they'll probably drop their price.

Left **A helpful concierge** Centre **Tipping etiquette** Right **Dress up well to eat out**

ㄒ10 Accommodation & Dining Tips

Hotel Taxes
The UAE is a tax-free country. However, visitors to the UAE can expect to pay a 10 per cent government tax and a 10 per cent service charge on hotel rooms.

Rooms
Hotel rooms in the UAE are spacious and also extremely secure. Most rooms are air-conditioned and come well equipped with television, telephones, minibar, tea and coffee facilities, toiletries and in-room safe. The best hotels also provide complimentary news-papers and bottled water.

Rack Rates & Discounts
While rack rates are quoted throughout this guide, they are rarely paid in the UAE. Travellers can book online through accommodation booking sites with considerably reduced discounts or book hotels as part of a package deal, while UAE residents can call hotels and request a residents discount.

Concierges
UAE concierges are generally excellent. They are a good source of local information and can recommend and book restaurants and organize transport and tours. They can also arrange to store your luggage if you have a late flight.

Extra costs
Extras that can add significantly to hotel room bills include phone calls and minibar costs. If you need to make lots of local phone calls, buy a local SIM card and phone card. While minibar prices are comparable to bar prices, you're better off buying duty free liquor.

Valet Parking
Almost all UAE hotels provide valet parking free-of-charge. Rarely will guests pay for valet parking if they're staying at a hotel, although there are exceptions. If you're staying in a mid-range or budget Deira hotel, you may have to park your car at a nearby parking station. The average cost is AED 20 per night. If you're hiring a car, contact your hotel ahead of time to enquire about parking facilities.

Tipping
In the UAE, it's customary to tip, although not obligatory. While most restaurants include a service charge, this doesn't always go to waiting staff. If the service was good, leave a tip, anything from 5–10 per cent. If it didn't meet your expectations, don't tip. Give porters a couple of dirhams per piece of luggage and if the taxi driver was friendly and helped with luggage, leave him a few coins.

Restaurant Reservations
Most hotels have "Restaurant Reservations" services. Take advantage of these to make your bookings, as there's nothing as tedious as having to visit half a dozen eateries before you find a table. Restaurants fill quickly in Dubai and Abu Dhabi and it can be hard to get a table on weekends. Make bookings as far in advance as possible.

Meal Times
UAE residents and locals eat late compared to North American, British and Australasian diners. Arab expats and Emiratis tend to book restaurant tables from 10pm onwards, while European expats eat around 8:30–9pm. Eat any earlier and you'll miss out on the fun – you'll only be dining with other tourists.

Dress Codes
Good restaurants require smart-casual to formal dress in the UAE. Emiratis wear their best *dishdashas* and *abayas*, while expats dress up too – even in casual restaurants, women will look glam while men will wear trousers (never jeans) and a long sleeved shirt. In fine dining restaurants, a smart suit jacket is expected (although a tie is sometimes optional).

Price Categories

For a standard, double room per night (with breakfast if included), taxes and extra charges.

D	Under AED 365
DD	AED 365-550
DDD	AED 550-730
DDDD	AED 730-1100
DDDDD	Over AED 1100

Ibis World Trade Centre lobby

Cheap Accommodation: Dubai

① Ibis World Trade Centre Hotel

One of Dubai's best bargains, the Ibis offers small, clean and stylish rooms. The catch, however, is that there's no service or extras for this price – don't expect someone to help with your bags. But there's Internet access, wireless in the public spaces, and the hotel restaurant, Cubo, offers decent Italian fare. ❀ *Map E6* • *Next to the Dubai Convention and Exhibition Centre, Sheikh Zayed Rd* • *04 332 4444* • *www. ibishotel.com* • *DD*

② Holiday Inn Express

This budget hotel is right in the middle of Dubai's media hub (Internet City, Media City and Knowledge Village) and makes a great base for exploring New Dubai. Rooms and facilities are generous for the price. ❀ *Map B2* • *Knowledge Village, New Dubai* • *04 427 5555* • *www.ichotelsgroup. com* • *DD*

③ Ahmedia Heritage Guesthouse

Book here for a real taste of heritage flavour. Located on the Deira side of the Creek, this guesthouse has spacious, traditionally styled rooms in a bright courtyard building. ❀ *Map K1* • *Near Al Ahmadiya School, Deira souq* • *04 225 0085* • *www.ahmedia guesthouse.com* • *DD*

④ easyHotel

The Jebel Ali easyHotel is a simple, no-frills establishment. Well located on the road out of Dubai towards Abu Dhabi, just a 10-minute taxi ride to the beaches, malls and restaurants of Dubai Marina. It's clean and well-maintained, and very cheap when a bed is all that matters. ❀ *Map A2* • *JAFZA* • *04 224 1777* • *www.easyhotel. com* • *D*

⑤ Capitol Hotel

Well-located on Mina Rd, this decent mid-range is ideal for those who want to experience it all – the old and new Dubai – and don't plan on spending much time at the hotel. If you do, you're in for nightclub noise and smoke even in the non-smoking rooms. ❀ *Map F4* • *Al Mina Rd, Satwa* • *04 346 0111* • *www. capitol-hotel.com* • *DD*

⑥ Pacific Hotel

Close to the shopping action of Deira's souqs and Baniyas Square, this budget hotel's simple rooms have satellite TV and balconies, but the main draw is the location. ❀ *Map L2* • *Al Sabkha Rd, Deira* • *04 227 6700* • *www.pacifichotel-dubai.com* • *DD*

⑦ Hotel Florida International

Situated in one of the most modern buildings in the area, this is also one of the cleanest of Deira's budget hotels. While the rooms are basic, they come with satellite TV. It's a short stroll away from Baniyas Square. ❀ *Map L1* • *Al Sabkha Rd, Deira* • *04 224 7777* • *www. florahospitality.com* • *D*

⑧ Ramee Hotel Apartments

In a bustling street of Bur Dubai, these spacious, clean hotel apartments are great value. They are equipped with satellite television and include kitchenettes with fridge, stovetop, microwave and washing machine. The undercover parking is an advantage in this area. ❀ *Map J2* • *Al Rolla Rd, Bur Dubai* • *04 352 2277* • *www. rameehotels.com* • *D*

⑨ Suha City Hotel

An economical offshoot of the boutique chain, Mondo. Excellent service, and centrally located behind Deira City Centre. Rooftop pool. ❀ *Map L5* • *Garhoud Rd, Deira* • *04 341 6111* • *www.suhacitydubai.com* • *DD*

⑩ Dubai Youth Hostel

Dubai's only youth hostel may not be central but it offers cheap and clean hotel-style accommodation in its new building, and basic dorm-like rooms in the old building. ❀ *Map F2* • *Al Nahda Rd, near Al Qusais* • *04 298 8161* • *www.uaeyha.com* • *D*

The budget hotels are mostly occupied with male traders. Women travelling unaccompanied may feel uncomfortable.

Streetsmart

Left **Novotel Centre Hotel** Centre **HJ Diplomat Hotel sign** Right **Loungers at Centro Yas Island**

Inexpensive Hotels: Abu Dhabi

Al Maha Arjaan
Ideally located on Hamdan Street in the centre, this green high-rise is great value and gets good reviews for service and cleanliness. 🕾 *Map P2 • Hamdan St • 02 610 6666 • www.rotana.com • DD*

Premier Inn
One of the cheapest options in town, this budget chain offers clean rooms and good facilities. It is located close to the beach and a short taxi ride from the centre. 🕾 *Abu Dhabi Capital Centre (next to Abu Dhabi National Exhibition Centre) • 02 813 1999 • www.premierinn.com • D*

Holiday Inn
Centrally-located hotel, well suited to a business stay. It has access to the Sheikh Zayed Mosque, and is 15 minutes away from the airport. 🕾 *2nd Street, off Airport Road • 02 657 4888 • www.ihg.com • DD*

Mercure Abu Dhabi Centre
Centrally located, this hotel looks worn around the edges and smells of smoke, but is popular with package tourists and airline crew. The low-ceilinged rooms can feel claustrophobic and the tiny windows don't take advantage of the views. 🕾 *Map P2 • Hamdan St • 02 633 3555 • www.accorhotels.com • DD*

Howard Johnson Diplomat Hotel
With several bars and clubs on site, this hotel sees a lot of action in the evenings, but it isn't really suitable for families. The spacious rooms are not particularly clean, but have good coffee-making facilities. It's also one of the few hotels in the city to allow pets. 🕾 *Map P4 • Khalifa St • 02 671 0000 • www.hojo.com • DD*

Grand Continental Flamingo Hotel
This shiny glass tower has shops and cinemas at its doorstep and the Corniche a couple of blocks away. The rooms are spacious and executive suites have kitchenettes. Rooms on high floors have fantastic views. Service, while efficient, can be impersonal. 🕾 *Map P2 • Hamdan St • 02 690 4000 • www.topgrandcontinentalflamingo.com • D*

Al Ain Palace Hotel
With the elegant Royal Meridien towering above it, you'd expect the Al Ain Palace to have an inferiority complex. Yet this friendly hotel is home to some of the best restaurants, making it an attractive option for those who don't feel like heading out after a hot day's sightseeing. 🕾 *Map N2 • Corniche Road East • 02 679 4777 • www.alainpalacehotel.com • DD*

Al Diar Capital Hotel
Slightly more upmarket than its nearby sister hotels, the Capital is nowhere near the quality you'd expect from the five-star classification it has. More of a mid-range business hotel, it represents a good deal only if you can get it for mid-range prices off the web or as part of a package. 🕾 *Map N1 • Meena Rd • 02 678 7700 • www.aldiarhotels.com • DDD*

Centro Yas Island
One of the first seven hotels to be built on Yas Island, the Centro is just minutes from the Yas Marina Formula 1 race track. Rooms are bright, modern and equipped with Wi-Fi access. The hotel is geared towards business travellers, but does have a restaurant, a bar and a swimming pool. 🕾 *Golf Plaza, Yas Island • 02 656 4444 • www.rotana.com • DDD*

Sands Hotel
A skyscraper hotel located bang in the centre of town, within walking distance of most landmarks. Rooms are clean, spacious and well-equipped, with tea-making facilities. There's a rooftop pool, a fitness centre, and a business centre. 🕾 *Map P2 • Sheik Zayed Rd/Electra St • 02 615 666 • www.danathotels.com • DD*

Price Categories

For a standard,	D	Under AED 365
double room per	DD	AED 365–550
night (with breakfast	DDD	AED 550–730
if included), taxes	DDDD	AED 730–1100
and extra charges.	DDDDD	Over AED 1100

Left **Traditional decor at the Orient Guest House** Right **The Rihab Rotana Suites emblem**

TOP 10 Mid-Priced Hotels: Dubai

XVA

This elegant hotel in a restored courtyard house is full of atmosphere. The stylish hotel rooms are minimalist in design. Don't expect any extras here; but who needs them when you can hear the call-to-prayer echoing through the streets? ◉ *Map K2 • Al Fahidi neighbourhood • 04 353 5383 • www.xvahotel.com • DDDD*

Al Bustan Rotana

The airport location seems to keep this outstanding five star hotel's pricing well below other hotels of similar quality. Rooms are spacious and well-equipped. The hotel is also home to some of the city's best eateries. ◉ *Map L6 • Garhoud, near Dubai International Airport • 04 282 0000 • www. rotana.com • DDDD*

Rihab Rotana

Five minutes from Dubai International Airport and a few minutes' walk from Deira City Centre mall, these sleek contem-porary suites on a busy road are ideal for business travellers and couples. The spacious rooms with well-equipped kitchenettes and all mod cons, are excellent value. If you can't face another meal out, there's a café downstairs. ◉ *Map L5 • Garhoud, next to City Centre • 04 294 0300 • www.rotana.com • DDDD*

Orient Guest House

This delightful boutique hotel is situated in a reno-vated courtyard building in the historic Al Fahidi neighbourhood. The traditional rooms with high ceilings are deco-rated in Arabian and Indian decor. The quiet courtyards are wonderful for relaxing in after a hot day's sightseeing. ◉ *Map K2 • Al Fahidi Roundabout, Bur Dubai • 04 351 9111 • www.orientguest house.com • DDD*

Villa 47

For those who prefer a B&B over a big hotel, this small guesthouse will please. Comfy rooms have en suite bathrooms, and balconies overhung by bougainvillea. Located in the quiet Garhoud area and convenient for the airport. ◉ *Map F2 • 19 St, Garhoud • 04 286 8239 • www.villa47.com • DD*

Four Points Sheraton

Conveniently located for Bur Dubai souqs, Dubai Museum, the Al Fahidi neighbourhood and Burjuman Mall shopping, this standard hotel is popular with business travellers and tourists on stopovers. ◉ *Map J2 • Khalid Bin Al-Waleed Rd • 04 397 7444 • www.four pointsburdubai.com • DDD*

Marco Polo Hotel

This excellent four-star may seem like it's off the beaten track, but

it's only a 10-minute taxi ride from the airport and a 15-minute stroll to the fascinating *dhow* wharves or Deira souqs. The hotel has a couple of excellent restaurants. ◉ *Map M2 • Al-Mateena St, Deira • 04 272 0000 • www. marcopolohotel.net • DDD*

Golden Sands Hotel Apartments

Comfortable self-catering in studios with kitchenettes, close to supermarkets and shops in Bur Dubai. All rooms have a TV and telephone. Free shuttle bus to Jumeirah. ◉ *Map J2 • Al Mankhool St, Bur Dubai • 04 355 5553 • www.golden sandsdubai.com • DD*

Regent Palace Hotel

Opposite the swish Burjuman shopping centre, this hotel has a great location. While the rooms are comfortable, they're in need of renovation. ◉ *Map J3 • Sheikh Khalifa Bin Zayed Rd, Bur Dubai • 04 396 3888 • www.rameehotels. com • DDDD*

Regal Plaza Hotel

A short stroll from Bur Dubai souqs, Dubai Museum and the Al Fahidi neighbourhood, and next door to electronics mall Al Ain. This hotel is fine if you're only after a bed for the night and don't mind a little noise. ◉ *Map J2 • Al Mankhool Rd, Bur Dubai • 04 355 6633 • www. rameehotels.com • DDDD*

Look online for the best deals on hotel rates.

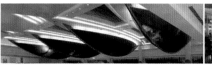

Left **Dhow bottoms in the Grand Hyatt Dubai ceiling** Right **The stunning Park Hyatt terrace**

TOP 10 Creek View Hotels: Dubai

1 Park Hyatt Dubai

This white Moroccan-inspired low-rise hotel is situated on one of the most sublime spots on Dubai Creek, overlooking the attractive marina and yacht club. ✪ *Map K5 • Dubai Creek Golf & Yacht Club, Deira • 04 602 1234 • www.dubai.park.hyatt. com • DDDDD*

2 InterContinental Dubai Festival City

The InterContinental at Dubai Festival City is a chic property, with superb attention to detail and well-drilled staff on hand throughout the hotel's vast amenities. Creek-view rooms have breathtaking vistas. ✪ *Map E3 • Dubai Festival City, Deira • 04 701 1111 • www.intercontinental. com • DDDDD*

3 Jumeirah Creekside Hotel

Furnished with modern art and contemporary designs, this wonderful hotel offers top-notch facilities, and gorgeous views of the creek. ✪ *Map L6 • Garhoud • 04 230 8555 • www.jumeirah. com • DDDDD*

4 Hilton Dubai Creek

Make sure to book a Creek view room for the best bird's-eye-view of Dubai's bustling waterway. This Carlos Ott-designed hotel is one of Dubai's most stylish, with a striking exterior and a sleek black marble interior. ✪ *Map L3 • Baniyas Rd, Deira • 04 227 1111 • www. hilton.com • DDDDD*

5 Grand Hyatt Dubai

This massive property may have marvellous views over Creekside Park across to the Dubai Creek Golf & Yacht Club, but it's easy to let the myriad attractions within the hotel distract you. There's a wonderful interior rainforest garden with *dhow* bottoms embedded in the ceiling and myriad bars and restaurants. ✪ *Map J6 • Al Qataiyat Rd, Bur Dubai • 04 317 1234 • www. dubai.grand.hyatt.com • DDDDD*

6 Radisson Blu Hotel

While the rooms here are comfortable, and there are Creek views from the small balconies, the design doesn't take advantage enough of its wonderful waterside location. ✪ *Map K2 • Baniyas Rd, Deira • 04 222 7171 • www. radissonblu.com • DDDDD*

7 Carlton Tower Hotel

With views of the Creek that are just as stunning as those from the Riviera next door, you'll pay more for a room at the Carlton because of its big swimming pool. And you probably won't regret it after a sweaty day in Dubai's heat. ✪ *Map L2 • Baniyas Rd, Deira • 04 222 7111 • www.carlton tower.net • DDDD*

8 Riviera Hotel

This is one of Dubai's best-located hotels for sightseeing. It's a short stroll to Deira's many souqs, while the fascinating *dhow* docks are just across the road. ✪ *Map K2 • Baniyas Rd, Deira • 04 222 1311 • www.rivierahotel-dubai. com • DDD*

9 Arabian Courtyard Hotel & Spa

The fine views from the Arabian Courtyard are some of Dubai's most fascinating. The Arabian-inspired rooms are spacious and the staff is friendly. ✪ *Map J2 • Al Fahidi St, opposite Dubai Museum, Bur Dubai • 04 351 9111 • www. arabiancourtyard.com • DDD*

10 Hyatt Regency

Stunningly situated on the waterfront promenade, the Hyatt Regency has spectacular views over the Arabian Sea. It has one of the most atmospheric lobbies, with palm trees, mashrabiya-screened balconies and glass feature floors with sand beneath them. ✪ *Map L1 • Al Khaleej Rd, Deira • 04 209 1234 • www.dubai.regency.hyatt. com • DD*

Left **The beach at the Meridien Mina Seyahi**

TOP 10 Luxury Beach Resorts: Dubai

Burj Al Arab

Dramatically jutting into the sea, Dubai's iconic, luxury property provides the ultimate in personal attention – from your arrival in a Rolls Royce, to the staff greeting you in the flamboyant foyer with welcome refreshments, cold towels, incense and dates, to the personal butler in your duplex suite. The interior is gaudy but the spectacular coastal views, especially from the Skyview Bar, make up for it *(see pp16–17)*.

One&Only Royal Mirage

One of the world's most romantic resorts, this is an exotic Moroccan-inspired hotel set in lush palm-filled gardens with serene ponds. The white sand beach is lined with elegant white umbrellas and regal private VIP canopies overlooking the Palm Island development *(see p44)*.

Al Qasr

The opulent Al Qasr ("the palace" in Arabic) is graced with enormous wooden doors, elegant arches and Moroccan stonework. You'll find mashrabiya screens, Moroccan lamps and terracotta urns all over the place. There's a gorgeous white sand beach and great views of Mina A'Salam and Burj Al Arab *(see pp18–19)*.

Mina A'Salam

The old-Arabian architecture of Mina A'Salam is inspired by the ancient towers of Yemen and Saudi Arabia as well as by the local wind-tower architecture of Dubai's Bastakiya area. The rooms feature rich upholsteries, inlaid furniture, Oriental lamps and Arabesque-patterned prints and tiles. The lattice balconies overlook the man-made waterways and splendid palm-lined beach *(see pp18–19)*.

Grosvenor House

The well-appointed rooms at this swanky hotel are spacious with stunning marina or sea views. Guests can use the white sand beach and access water activities at its sister hotel across the road, the Royal Meridien. ✆ *Map B2 • Dubai Marina • 04 399 8888 • www.grosvenor house-dubai.com • DDDDD*

Ritz Carlton

This sumptuous hotel lives up to the reputation of this renowned chain, with lots of marble, chandeliers, Persian carpets and fresh flowers everywhere. Its palm-filled gardens and white sand beach are outstanding *(see p44)*.

Le Meridien Mina Seyahi Resort

Indulge in a wide range of beach activities and water sports from wind surfing and wakeboarding to sailing and deep-sea fishing. There are several swimming pools and also a complimentary kid's "Penguin Club" *(see p44)*.

Jumeirah Beach Hotel

While the interiors of this wave-shaped hotel are rather gaudy when compared with Dubai's chic new hotels, families love the bright, bold colours, excellent beach facilities and myriad kids' activities *(see p44)*.

Westin Mina Seyahi

This elegant addition to Dubai's five-star coastline boasts spectacular views over the Arabian Gulf. The beautifully appointed rooms are spacious and well-equipped; some, but not all have balconies. Other facilities include a spa, gym, several bars and restaurants and an excellent watersports centre *(see p45)*.

Atlantis, The Palm

Located at the top of the Palm Jumeirah, this vast complex has a wide choice of rooms, most with views over the gulf. The ultimate in luxury, however, are the Lost Chambers suites with underwater views into the lagoon. Among the many facilities are a waterpark, a dolphinarium and a kids' club, making it ideal for families *(see p44)*.

Left **Emirates Palace** Centre **Millennium Hotel lobby** Right **Le Royal Meridien swimming pool**

TOP 10 Luxury Resorts: Abu Dhabi

Emirates Palace
Choose from amongst the Coral, Pearl and Diamond Rooms, Khaleej Suites or Palace Suites. All the rooms feature wide plasma TVs and extras such as welcome cocktails, flowers and fruit in the room, butler service, complimentary minibar and Internet access (see pp22–3).

Le Royal Meridien
While all the rooms are beautifully appointed and have sublime views of the Corniche and Arabian Sea, the Royal Club rooms are worth the extra dirhams for the Hermès products alone. ⬡ Map N2 • Khalifa St • 02 674 2020 • www.leroyalmeridienabudhabi.com • DDDDD

Shangri-La Qaryat Al Beri
The Shangri-La is a superb hotel with rooms overlooking either the long private beach, or one of the swimming pools. It also has a spa, restaurants and a shopping centre. ⬡ Qaryat Al Beri • 02 509 8888 • www.shangri-la.com • DDDDD

Fairmont Bab al Bahr
With 369 sumptuous rooms and views over the Creek and Grand Mosque, this sleek five-star hotel is surprisingly homely. All rooms have LCD TVs and lavish bathrooms, plus there's a fitness centre and a private beach. Chef Marco Pierre White has made his mark here with two restaurants. ⬡ Between the Bridges • 02 654 3333 • www.fairmont.com/babalbahr • DDDDD

Millennium Hotel
This swanky hotel has elegant expansive rooms with splendid views over the Corniche and Lulu Island and out to sea. Ideally positioned for sightseeing, the small swimming pool is a disappointment. ⬡ Map N2 • Khalifa St • 02 614 6000 • www.millenniumhotels.com • DDDDD

Le Meridien
The rooms here are very plush, with velvet upholstery and dark wood. The interactive TVs and high-speed Internet make this hotel ideal for business travellers. The highlight, however, is the Meridien Village, with 15 restaurants and bars set in lush tropical gardens. ⬡ Map P1 • Tourist Club area • 02 644 6666 • www.lemeridienabudhabi.com • DDDD

Sheraton Abu Dhabi Resort & Towers
There are good water and leisure activities here and the beachside sheesha spot is lovely. Eat at the excellent restaurants on site. ⬡ Map N1 • Corniche Rd East, Tourist Club area • 02 677 3333 • www.sheraton.com/abudhabi • DDDDD

Anantara Qasr Al Sarab
This unique fortress-style resort sits majestically in the middle of the desert. The rooms feature five-star luxuries and there are private villas, each with a pool and butler service, too. ⬡ A 90-minute drive from Abu Dhabi • 02 886 2088 • www.anantara.com • DDDDD

Hilton Abu Dhabi
Long a favourite of Abu Dhabi's expats for its excellent restaurants and bars, holidaymakers love the hotel's beautiful swimming pools and Breakwater beach, lined with shady palm trees, and myriad water sports. Rooms are spacious and comfortable and come with many little extras. ⬡ Map P6 • Corniche Rd West • 02 681 1900 • www.hilton.com • DDDD

Park Hyatt Abu Dhabi
Located on a 9-km (6-mile) stretch of beach, with its very own landscaped garden, the Park Hyatt has become one of Abu Dhabi's most desired locations. It is just a short drive from the city, but a world away in terms of tranquility. ⬡ Saadiyat Island • 02 407 1234 • www.abudabi.parkhyatt.com • DDDDD

 Business travellers should ask hotels for corporate rates, which are considerably less than rack rates.

Price Categories

For a standard, double room per night (with breakfast if included), taxes and extra charges.	**D**	Under AED 365
	DD	AED 365–550
	DDD	AED 550–730
	DDDD	AED 730–1100
	DDDDD	Over AED 1100

Left **Kempinski Hotel reception** Right **The Thai experience at Dusit Dubai**

TOP 10 Business & City Hotels: Dubai

Raffles Dubai

The Middle East's first Raffles combines warmth and luxury with impeccable service. Its enormous rooms have great views from the distinctive Egyptian-style pyramid building, which gels with the Wafi shopping complex. The hotel's restaurant, Fire & Ice *(see p71)*, has become one of the city's best. ✎ *Map H6 • Sheikh Rashis Rd • 04 324 8888 • www.raffles.com • DDDD*

Jumeirah Emirates Towers

This elegant hotel's lobby is one of the city's most vibrant, especially in the evenings. Adjoining the hotel is the chic Boulevard shopping centre with excellent eateries and bars *(see p36).*

Kempinski Hotel

A contemporary city style hotel, it offers a swish alternative to the beach resorts. The hotel is attached to Mall of the Emirates' indoor snow park, Ski Dubai *(see p32)*. The well-equipped rooms are spacious and very swanky. ✎ *Map C2 • Sheikh Zayed Rd, Interchange 4, Al Barsha • 04 347 0000 • www.kempinski.com • DDDDD*

Radisson Blu Dubai Media City

This smart hotel in the centre of Dubai Media City is ideal for those doing business here or for tourists looking for an alternative to the beach experience – Dubai Marina, Mall of the Emirates and Ibn Battuta Mall are nearby. ✎ *Map B2 • Dubai Media City • 04 366 9111 • www.radissonblu.com • DDDDD*

Dusit Thani

What sets the Dusit apart is its gentle welcoming Thai hospitality, from the "Sawadee-ka" greeting to the Thai canapés. The spacious rooms cater well to the business traveller, but it's worth paying extra for Club Rooms, which come with enticing perks. ✎ *Map C6 • Sheikh Zayed Rd • 04 343 3333 • www.dusit.com • DDDDD*

Fairmont

Conveniently located for business, shopping and sightseeing, the hotel's architecture and plush rooms ooze elegance and style. ✎ *Map E5 • Sheikh Zayed Rd • 04 332 5555 • www.fairmont.com • DDDD*

Shangri-La

Known as the hotel where Hollywood's stars choose to stay – George Clooney and Matt Damon did so when making the movie *Syriana* – this is one of Dubai's swankiest, with a dramatic lobby, posh rooms and splendid restaurants. ✎ *Map C5 • Sheikh Zayed Rd • 04 343 8888 • www.shangri-la.com • DDDDD*

The Address Downtown

While its 63 storeys may pale in comparison to its neighbour, the Burj tower, this elegant and modern hotel still offers impressive views of the city. The hotel's attention to detail is evident in the stylish guestrooms while the outstanding facilities include a spa, fitness centre and seven gourmet restaurants. ✎ *Map C6 • Downtown Burj Khalifa • 04 436 8888 • www.theaddress.com • DDDDD*

The Palace

Adjoining the Souk Al Bahar is this luxurious offering. Facilities include three international restaurants, a spa and excellent business facilities. Despite its proximity to the busy Dubai Mall and Dubai Fountain, a stay here is a calm and tranquil experience. ✎ *Map C6 • Downtown Burj Khalifa • 04 428 7888 • www.theaddress.com • DDDDD*

Al Murooj Rotana Hotel & Suites

This is a popular Mediterranean-style hotel. Regular guests like the comfortable rooms and personable but professional service, while expats have taken a liking to the many relaxed restaurants and cafés on site. ✎ *Map D6 • Just off Sheikh Zayed Rd near Defence Roundabout • 04 321 1111 • www.rotana.com • DDDDD*

"Club" rooms come with extras such as use of the "Club Lounge", meeting rooms, afternoon tea, pre-dinner drinks and canapés.

General Index

Index

Index

Acknowledgements

The Authors

LARA DUNSTON was an Abu Dhabi resident of five years and Dubai resident of three. Lara has authored several guides to Dubai and the UAE, and scores of travel features for magazines and newspapers around the world.

SARAH MONAGHAN lived in Dubai for five years where she edited its leading glossy women's magazine, *Emirates Woman*. The former editor of *Everything Spain Magazine* and currently of *Gabon Magazine*, she now contributes travel features to national and international publications.

TERRY CARTER specializes in travel photography and his work has featured in guidebooks and magazines across the globe. A former Dubai and Abu Dhabi resident, he's often back shooting in these cities and loves the clear light and friendliness of the multicultural population.

AT DORLING KINDERSLEY

Publisher
Douglas Amrine

Publishing Manager
Sadie Smith

Design Manager
Jane Ewart

Project Art Editor
Sonal Bhatt

Senior Cartographic Designers
Casper Morris, Suresh Kumar

Cartographer
Jasneet Kaur

DTP Designer
Natasha Lu

Production
Rita Sinha

Photographer
Terry Carter

Fact checking
Debbie Rooke

Additional Photography
Sonal Bhatt, Peter Cornelissen

Revisions Team
Caroline Elliker, Anna Freiberger, Rhiannon Furbear, Camilla Gersh, Lydia Halliday, Bharti Karakoti, Sumita Khatwani, Maite Lantaron, Nicola Malone, Alison McGill, Marianne Petrou, Alex Ritman, Avantika Sukhia, Gavin Thomas, David Tombesi-Walton, Ajay Verma, Matt Warnock

Maps
Base mapping for Dubai City, Greater Dubai and Abu Dhabi derived from Netmaps.

Key:
a-above; b-below/bottom; c-centre; f-far; l-left; r-right; t-top.

The photographer, writers and publisher would like to thank the media staff at the following sights and organizations for their helpful cooperation:

One&Only Royal Mirage; Jumeirah International; Emirates Palace and Kempinski Mall of the Emirates; Grosvenor House, Le Royal Meridien, Meridien, Sheraton Hotels and Starwood Group; Radisson Blu Dubai Media City and Deira Hotels; Park Hyatt Dubai, Grand Hyatt Dubai and Hyatt International; Fairmont Hotel; Dusit Dubai; Arabian Courtyard Hotel and Spa; Marco Polo Hotel; Al Tayer Group; The Rotana Group, Abu Dhabi Beach Rotana, Al Maha Rotana and

Dubai Towers Rotana Hotel; Abu Dhabi Millennium Hotel; Sho Cho and Dubai Marine Beach Resort and Spa; Zinc at the Crowne Plaza Hotel; Wafi City & Cleopatra's Spa; Sheikh Mohammed Centre for Cultural Understanding; Dubai Museum; Abu Dhabi Cultural Foundation; Arabian Adventures; Ski Dubai; Time Machine Group; Luca Gagliardi and Gordon Ramsey's Verre; Sheikh Maisa Al Qassimi and the Amzaan staff; The Third Line; 9714; Gallery I.V.D.E.; Basta Art Cafe; XVA; Art Space; Lata's; Mumbai Se; Ginger and Lace; Villa Moda; National Iranian Carpets; Pride of Kashmir; Al Jaber Gallery; Anita Daga and InterContinental Hotel Group; Mark Fuller and Embassy; and Stephanie Khouy and Raffles Dubai.

4CORNERSIMAGES: SIME/ Schmid Reinhard 56-7; ALDAR PROPERTIES PJSC: 32tr; ALAMY: G P Bowater 54b; Jon Arnold Images: Gavin Hellier 1c; Eric Nathan 7cra; ASDA'A BURSON-MARSTELLER: Nigel Brand 48tr; ATLANTIS, KERZNER INTERNATIONAL RESORTS INC.: 45tl; 85tc.
BALLOON ADVENTURES DUBAI: 50br; NAKHEEL BRANDHUB: 32b; BURJ KHALIFA: Emmar Properties 33tr.

CORBIS: Georgina Bowater 28-9; Jose Fuste Raga 6bc; 4-5; 86-7.

DALMA MALL: 37tl; DUBAI AUTODROME LLC: 50tr; DUBAI AQUARIUM & UNDERWATER ZOO: 52tl; DUBAI GOLF: 65tl.

EMAAR: 72cl.

GETTY IMAGES: The Image Bank/ Martin Child 88tr; Hugh Sitton 3br.

HEMISPHERE DESIGN STUDIO & GALLERY: 35tl; HILTON WORLDWIDE: 63tl.

JUMEIRAH IMAGE LIBRARY: 37tl, 43bl.

KEMPINSKI HOTELS: 42cra.

LEONARDO MEDIABANK: 93tl.

LE MERIDIEN DUBAI: 116tr.

ROTANA HOTEL MANAGEMENT CORPORATION LTD: 112tr; LE ROYAL MERIDIEN ABU DHABI: 95tl.

SIR BANI YAS & SAADIYAT ISLAND: © TDIC 32tl, 32tc.

JOHN WEISS: © www.tsca.net, 2003 10cla.

All other images © Dorling Kindersley.

For further information see: www.dkimages.com.

Special Editions of DK Travel Guides

Phrase Book

In an Emergency

Help!	Enje**dooni**
Stop	**Wak**-kaf
Can you call a doctor?	**Mom**kin **tat**lob tabeeb?
Can you call an ambulance?	**Mom**kin **tat**lob el es'**aaf**?
Can you call the police?	**Mom**kin **tat**lob el **shor**ta?
Can you call the fire brigade?	**Mom**kin **tat**lob el etfaa?
Where is the nearest hospital?	Wayn **ag**rab mos**tash**fa?
Is there a telephone here?	Ako tele**foon huna?**

Useful Words and Phrases

Yes	**Na**-am
No	Laa
Hello	Sa**laam** a**lai**kum
Goodbye	**Ma**'aa al sa**laama**
See you later	**Ela** al le**kaa**
Excuse me	**'Af**wan
Sorry (said by man)	**Aa**sif
Sorry (said by woman)	**Aa**sifa
Thank you	Shake**reen**
Please	Luw **tas**ma'h
Peace be upon you	Al sa**laam** '**a**laikum
Peace be upon you (as response)	A**lai**kum al sa**laam**
Good morning	Sa**baa**'h al khayr
Good evening	Ma**saa**-o al khayr
Good night	Tosbi**hoo**na **a**la khayr
Pleased to meet you	Ya ah**leen**
How are you?	Keef al 'haal?
I'm fine	Zeen
I don't understand	Ma **af**ham
What did he say?	**She**nu kaal?
Do you speak English?	**Ta**'hki enk**leezi**?
Does anyone speak English?	**Aku** '**ha**da ye'h**kee** enk**leezi**?
Have you got a table for…?	**Aku taa**wila hug …?
I would like to reserve a table	A**reed a'h**jiz **taa**wila
Can I have the bill please?	Al 'he**saab** luw **tas**ma'h
I am vegetarian	**Ana** na**baa**ti
God willing	In**shaal**-la
No problem	**Maa**fi **mosh**kila
big	ka**beer**
small	sa**geer**
hot	'**haar**
cold	**baa**nid
bad	say-**ye**'e
good	tay-**yeb**
open	maf**too**'h
closed	me**sak**-kar
on the right	'**ala** al ya**meen**
on the left	'**ala** al ya**saar**
near	ka**reeb**
far	ba'**eed**
men's toilet	twa**let** hug al re**jaal**
ladies' toilet	twa**let** hug al '**ha**reem
a little	ka**leel**
a lot	**waa**jed

Making a Telephone Call

Hello	A**loo**
I'd like to speak to…	A**reed** akal-**lim** …
This is…	**Ana** …
I'll call back later	**Raa**'h at-ta**sel** ba'a**deen**
Please say … called	Khab-**bir**ho **an**-na … et-ta**sal**

In a Hotel

hotel	**fon**dok
Do you have a room?	La**day**kom '**hoj**ra?
I have a reservation	**En**di 'hajz
With bathroom	Bee 'ham-**maam**
single room	'**hoj**ra far**diy**-ya
double room	'**hoj**ra le et**neen**
porter	na**toor**
shower	dosh
key	mef**taa**'h

Sightseeing

art gallery	**ma'a**rad luw'**haat** faney-ya
beach	**shaate**'e
bus station	**muw**gaf el **baah**s
district	**men**takaa
entrance	**mad**khal
exit	**makh**raj
garden	'**hadee**ka
guide	**mor**shid
guided tour	**mor**shid al **juw**la
map	**khaar**ta
mosque	**jaam**e'a
museum	**mut**'haf
park	mota**naz**-zah
river	**na**her
taxi	**tak**si
ticket	**tath**kara
tourist office	**mak**tab se**yaa**'hi
Please put the (taxi) meter on	Luw **tas**ma'h, **daw**-war al '**ad**-daad
How much is it to…?	Kam raah te**kal**-lafni **e**la …?
Please take me to (this address)	**Khoth**ni e**la** (**haa**za al 'on**waan**)

Shopping

How much is it?	Kam floos?
I'd like…	A**reed**
This one	**Haa**za
Do you accept credit cards?	Hal takba**loon kre**dit kaard?
That's too much	**Haa**za **waa**yed
I'll give you…	**Ana** raa'h a'a**teek** …
I'll take it	Raa'h **aakh**doh
market	sook
expensive	**ghaa**li
cheap	ra**khees**
chemist's	sayda**laa**ni

Menu Decoder

'aish	rice
'a**seer**	fruit juice
be**doon**	without
bee	with
beera	beer
beez	egg
beez mas**look**	hard-boiled egg
ber**iaan**i al da**jaaj**	chicken biryani
ber**iaan**i al **la**hem	meat biryani
ber**iaan**i al robi**aan**	shrimp biryani

When you see an ' in the Arabic, this means that you pronounce the letter after it with a little puff of air.

iberiaani samak	fish biryani (with bones)
ibolti	spiced tilapia (fish) grilled and served whole
ida-en	mutton
idajaaj	chicken
ifaakiha	fruit
ifalaafel	vegetarian burger made with chickpeas
ifee al forn	roasted
ifulful	white pepper
ifulful aswad	black pepper
igabgab	steamed crab
iguhwa	bitter Arabic coffee
ihaleeb	milk
ihalwa	Turkish delight with cardamom
iham-moor	local fish that tastes like snapper
iham-moor magli	deep-fried hammoor
iharees	gruel cooked in beef stock
iheel	cardamom
iholo	sweet
ikabaab	kebab
ikabsa	dish of rice, meat/chicken, dried lemon and saffron
ikabsat dajaaj	dish of rice, chicken, dry lemon and saffron
ikabsat lahem	dish of rice, meat, dry lemon and saffron
ikereem	cream
ikhal	vinegar made from molasses
ikhamr	wine
ikhoboz	bread
ikhoboz jabaab	large spiced pancakes with cardamom
ikhoboz shaami	pita bread
ikhoboz tost	toast
ikofta	grilled meatballs
ikoozi	lamb
ikoskos	plain couscous
imaglee	fried
imalh	salt
imarag	spiced meat/chicken stock
imarag dajaaj	chicken stock
imarag lahem	beef stock
imashroob ghaazi	soft drink
imashwi	grilled
imashwi ala el fa'hm	barbecued over coal
imasloog	boiled
imohal-li senaa-ee	sweetener
inoham-mas	toasted
inabeez	wine
ineskafee	coffee
iorz	rice
iorz bil zafaraan	rice with saffron
irobyaan	large grilled shrimp
ishai	tea
ishawirma	doner kebab
isuk-kar	sugar
isulsa	tomato purée cooked in stock
tahye motawas-sit	medium
shaaw meen dajaaj	chicken chowmein
shaaw meen lahem	beef chowmein
tshaaw meen samak	seafood chowmein
tshoop sooy	chop suey
wajba khafeefa	snack
zaatar	thyme
tangabeel	ginger powder
zobod	butter

Numbers

1	waa'hid
2	etneen
3	thalaatha
4	arba'aa
5	khamsa
6	sit-ta
7	saba'a
8	thamaaneya
9	tes'aa
10	'ashra
11	'hedaash
12	etnaash
13	talat-taash
14	arba'-taash
15	khamastaash
16	sit-taash
17	saba'ataash
18	tamantaash
19	tesa'ataash
20	eshreen
21	waa'hid wa eshreen
30	thalatheen
40	arbe'een
50	khamseen
60	sit-teen
70	sab'een
80	thamaneen
90	tes'een
100	me-aa
1000	alf

Time

Today	el yoom
yesterday	el barha
tomorrow	baaker
morning	sabaa'h
afternoon	zaheera
evening	masaa
night	lail
now	al 'heen
tonight	el laila
minute	dageega
hour	sa'aa
week	osboo'a
month	shahr
year	'aam

Days of the Week

Monday	al ethneen
Tuesday	al thulathaa
Wednesday	al arbe'a
Thursday	al khamees
Friday	al jomo'aa
Saturday	al sabet
Sunday	al a'had

Months

January	yanaayer
February	febraayer
March	maars
April	abreel
May	maayo
June	yonyo
July	yolyo
August	agostos
September	sebtamber
October	oktoobar
November	noovambir
December	deesambir

Selected Street Index